ONE-MINUTE WEEKLY SPORTS DEVOTIONS FOR FEMALE ATHLETES

CHRISTIAN INSPIRATION FOR TEEN GIRLS TO BUILD FAITH AND MENTAL TOUGHNESS, CRUSH PRESSURE, LEAD WITH CONFIDENCE & PLAY WITH PURPOSE

NEXTLEVEL PUBLICATIONS

CONTENTS

BONUS: FUEL YOUR FAITH

DOWNLOAD YOUR FREE GUIDES BELOW

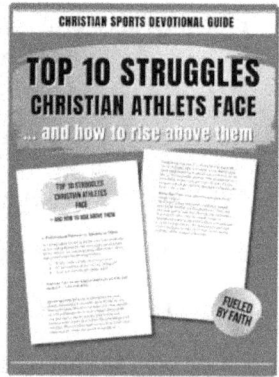

GAME PLAN FOR GROWTH

Greatness doesn't just belong to the guys. Today's female athletes are breaking barriers—and the strongest ones know where their real power comes from. Katie Ledecky is the most decorated U.S. female swimmer, yet she humbly points every medal back to God. Gabby Douglas stood on the Olympic stage with the world watching and boldly gave Him the glory. Alyssa Naeher trusted God's strength when the pressure of the World Cup was on her shoulders. Jennie Finch dominated the softball field but made her biggest impact by sharing her faith with the next generation of girls.

What made them shine wasn't just talent. It was **courage fueled by faith, resilience through setbacks, humility in victory, and confidence rooted in Christ.** That's exactly what this devotional is designed to build in you.

One-Minute Weekly Sports Devotions for Female Athletes is your weekly faith workout—simple but powerful lessons designed for **female teen athletes ages 10–18** who want to grow in faith and live with purpose. Just like reps in the gym build muscle, these one-minute devotions will build lasting confidence, mental toughness, humility, and integrity—the strength that carries you through games, practices, school, friendships, and life.

Here's how each week is laid out:

- **Victory Verse** — A powerful Scripture to set the tone for your week.

- **Beyond the Scoreboard** — A short, game-ready lesson featuring real stories from professional female Christian athletes and teams who've faced pressure, setbacks, and comebacks.

- **Game Plan for Growth** — Reflection questions, journaling space, and a challenge to apply the lesson to your sport and your life.

- **Faith Huddle** — A quick, focused prayer to realign your heart and goals with God.

With just a few minutes each week, you'll learn how to:

- **Play with purpose**

- **Build unshakable confidence**

- **Handle pressure and comparisons with peace**

- **Develop mental toughness rooted in Christ**

- **Lead boldly with Christ-like character**

Your sport is a gift—but your influence is even greater. So lace up, dig deep, and train your heart like you train your body—with passion, purpose, and the power of God's Word.

SECTION 1:
FOUNDATIONS OF FAITH

(WEEKS 1 - 16)

This section helps you to anchor your identity in Christ and understand your greater purpose beyond the stats. Before you can lead on the field, you must be anchored in who you are off it. These first devotions equip young female athletes with guidance on how to strengthen their identity in Christ, encourage self-love, embrace humility and gratitude, and compete with unwavering integrity—laying the spiritual groundwork for a life and game that glorifies God.

CHAPTER 1: IMAGE & IDENTITY

1

FEARFULLY & WONDERFULLY MADE

"I praise you because I am fearfully and wonderfully made; your works are wonderful, I know that full well."
Psalm 139:14

BEYOND THE SCOREBOARD

Lesson: When Olympic swimmer **Missy Franklin** first burst onto the world stage, she didn't just battle competitors in the pool—she also battled comparisons. At 6'2" with powerful shoulders, her body didn't fit the world's idea of "feminine perfection." Like many young female athletes face today, the media comments, social pressures, and self-criticism could have crushed Missy's confidence and self-image. Yet Missy made a bold choice: she refused to let the world's standards define her. Instead, she anchored her identity in Christ. Missy often shared that her self-worth came from the Lord, not from medals, headlines, or appearance. Even as one of the most decorated swimmers in history, she wanted young girls to know their worth is not tied to how they look or how others see them. Missy's self-confidence flowed from understanding Psalm 139:14—that God knit her together with strength and uniqueness on purpose. For her, broad, muscular shoulders weren't a flaw. They were a gift that helped her excel in swimming and glorify God through her sport.

It's easy to feel pressure "to fit in" and get caught up in comparisons—body image, popularity, or how we "look" in uniform. Social media, uniform and accessory equipment, and body comparisons all whisper lies that your value depends on appearance. God's Word crushes that lie. Psalm 139 reminds us that God designed every detail of who we are. Strength, height, muscle, and grit are not flaws. They're features crafted for a purpose. Your self-worth should be unshakable because it rests in His design, not in anyone else's approval.

GAME PLAN FOR GROWTH

Reflection: *Where do I feel the most pressure to compare myself to others in my sport? What truth from Psalm 139 can I remind myself of this week?*

_____

_____

_____

Challenge: This week, reject comparison by writing down three strengths that God gave you on a note and stick it on your mirror. When you catch yourself comparing to other female athletes, read them out loud. Compete with confidence that your Creator designed you exactly as He intended. Remember, God doesn't make mistakes.

FAITH HUDDLE

Prayer: Thank You, Lord, for creating me with strength, beauty, and purpose. Help me stop comparing myself to others and to remember that I am wonderfully made in Your image. Anchor my worth in You alone. **Amen.**

2

FIX YOUR EYES

"Let us fix our eyes on Jesus, the author and perfecter of our faith."
Hebrews 12:2

BEYOND THE SCOREBOARD

Lesson: At just 15 years old, **Coco Gauff** became one of the youngest players to ever compete at Wimbledon and win a Grand Slam. Overnight, she went from being a teenager with a normal life to having millions of people analyzing her game, her appearance, and even her personality. With that fame came a flood of social media attention—praise when she won, criticism when she lost, and endless comparisons to other athletes. Coco admitted that scrolling through Instagram likes, comments, and highlight reels quickly drained her confidence and self-worth.

Instead of letting online strangers shape how she saw herself, Coco chose to step back from social media platforms. Coco has openly shared how she learned to limit her time on social media and guard her heart from comparison. Rather than letting comments or follower counts define her, she chose to focus on what really matters: her faith in Christ and the joy of competing with purpose. Coco's self-confidence doesn't come from fitting an online image. It comes from fixing her eyes on Jesus, who never changes how He sees her.

For female athletes today, social media comparisons can feel impossible to escape. Scrolling through Instagram or TikTok, it's easy to feel "less than"— less talented, less pretty, or less popular. But Hebrews 12:2 calls us to a different focus: to fix our eyes on Jesus. When your focus is on Him, the noise of comparison fades. The more we look to Him for self-worth, the less we're distracted by what's happening on a screen. Your value is no longer determined by likes, comments, or highlight reels. Rather, it's rooted in the unwavering truth that Christ made you, loves you, and has a purpose for you.

GAME PLAN FOR GROWTH

Reflection: *How does social media affect the way I see myself? Where am I most tempted to compare myself to others online?*

Challenge: Choose one boundary for your social media use this week. Whether it's limiting screen time, unfollowing comparison accounts, or replacing a scroll session with an uplifting prayer. Each time you're tempted to compare, recite the words of Hebrews 12:2 and point your focus back to Christ.

FAITH HUDDLE

Prayer: Thank You, God, for reminding me that my value and worth are not found online. Help me guard my heart from comparison and keep my eyes fixed on You. Shape my focus so that my self-confidence comes from Your truth. **Amen.**

3

ENOUGH IN CHRIST

"Am I now trying to win the approval of human beings, or of God? Or am I trying to please people? If I were still trying to please people, I would not be a servant of Christ."
Galatians 1:10

BEYOND THE SCOREBOARD

Lesson: Beach volleyball icon **Kerri Walsh Jennings** is one of the most accomplished athletes in Olympic history, with three gold medals and a reputation as one of the fiercest competitors in the game. Yet behind the victories, she has often shared that she struggled with the heavy pressure to be perfect—perfect in her performance, her training, and even her image as a role model. The world expected her to always win, always lead, and always deliver. Carrying that weight nearly crushed her.

Kerri eventually learned that chasing perfection and the approval of others left her feeling empty. What freed her from this burden was shifting her focus from people's expectations to God's truth. Galatians 1:10 reminds us that we can't live to always please people and truly serve Christ at the same time. Kerri realized that no amount of gold medals or praise could ever satisfy the constant need for approval. When she began to center her identity in God—not in what others thought—she found that the weight of the burden lifted. Playing for His approval gave her the strength to compete without the fear of failure. Her worth wasn't tied to flawless performance, but to the One who loved her even in her mistakes.

It's easy to fall into the trap of people-pleasing and perfectionism. Female athletes often feel like their worth depends on never making mistakes, being perfect, making everyone happy, or proving they belong. But perfection isn't the goal—faithfulness is. Galatians 1:10 calls us to stop chasing the approval of others and anchor our identity in Christ. Like Kerri, you don't have to carry the burden of being perfect and pleasing everyone. You can step onto the court or field knowing that you are already enough in Christ.

GAME PLAN FOR GROWTH

Reflection: *Where do I feel the strongest pressure to be perfect? Whose approval am I chasing the most—friends, teammates, coaches, or parents?*

_____

_____

_____

Challenge: Before every practice or game this week, whisper to yourself: *"I play for God's approval, not people's."* Write Galatians 1:10 in your notebook, locker, or on your water bottle to remind yourself that you're already enough in Christ.

FAITH HUDDLE

Prayer: Thank You, Lord, that I don't have to be perfect or please everyone to be loved by You. Help me release the weight of people's expectations and play for Your approval alone. Remind me daily that I am enough in Christ. **Amen.**

4

LOVED AS I AM

"For we are God's handiwork, created in Christ Jesus to do good works, which God prepared in advance for us to do."
Ephesians 2:10

BEYOND THE SCOREBOARD

Lesson: Tamika Catchings is one of the greatest players in WNBA history, but her journey to stardom started with struggle. Born with hearing loss and a speech impediment, Tamika wore hearing aids that made her feel different from everyone else. As a child, she was teased for the way she spoke and often felt ashamed of who she was. At times, Tamika wished she could rip out her hearing aids and toss them aside, believing life would be easier if she just blended in. Loving herself felt impossible.

But over time, Tamika began to see her challenges differently. Through basketball, she discovered strong determination, work ethic, and resilience—qualities that would make her a basketball champion. More importantly, through her faith, she realized her image and identity weren't a mistake. Ephesians 2:10 reminded her that she was God's handiwork, crafted with intention and purpose. What once felt like flaws became the very tools God used to shape her character and inspire others with similar disabilities. Tamika used these strengths to connect with people, be resilient, and "see plays before they happened." She chose to view her differences through God's lens, not the world's.

For many female athletes, the toughest opponent isn't across the net or on the field. It's the voice inside that says you'll never measure up. But Ephesians 2:10 tells us something more powerful. You are His handiwork, and you are enough. He designed you on purpose, and every detail of your life can be used for His plan. Self-love doesn't mean pride—it means embracing who God made you to be and walking in the confidence of His design. Similar to Tamika, you can learn to love yourself not because you're flawless, but because you're His creation, loved as you are.

GAME PLAN FOR GROWTH

Reflection: *What part of myself do I struggle the most to love? What are my unique strengths can I thank God for today? What is one way I can practice healthy self-love this week?*

Challenge: Each morning this week, write one thing you appreciate about how God made you. Keep the list where you can see it—on your mirror, locker, or notebook. Let it remind you daily that you are loved as you are, God's masterpiece created with purpose.

FAITH HUDDLE

Prayer: Heavenly Father, thank You for creating me with care and intention. Help me replace self-doubt with self-love rooted in Your truth. Teach me to see myself as Your masterpiece and to walk in confidence with the purpose You prepared for me. **Amen.**

5

BEYOND THE LABELS

"The Lord does not look at the things people look at. People look at the outward appearance, but the Lord looks at the heart."
1 Samuel 16:7

BEYOND THE SCOREBOARD

Lesson: Cheerleading often comes with unfair stereotypes. Many assume it's just about looks, style, or performance instead of strength, resilience, discipline, and leadership. **Reece Weaver**, a professional cheerleader for the Dallas Cowboys and outspoken Christian, knows this pressure first-hand. Throughout her career, she's faced the labels the world tries to attach to cheerleaders—judgments about appearance, assumptions about worth, and dismissals of the hard work behind the sport.

Reece has spoken out publicly about refusing to let those labels define her. She reminds young athletes that identity doesn't come from how others categorize you, but from who God says you are. 1 Samuel 16:7 echoes this truth. People may focus on outward appearance, but God looks at the heart. When Samuel was sent to anoint Israel's next king, even he was tempted to choose based on looks. But God makes it very clear. What matters is not the surface, but the spirit inside.

As a female athlete, labels and stereotypes can feel crushing. Maybe you've been called "too girly" to be taken seriously, "too muscular" to be feminine, or "just a cheerleader." But God doesn't see those labels. He sees your heart, your character, and the gifts He placed in you. Like Reece, you can rise above stereotypes by embracing God's perspective. Your worth isn't in a title, a uniform, or an opinion—it's in being His chosen daughter. The world may try to define you by labels that shift and fade over time, but God's truth and love never change. When you live from His view of who you are, no label or stereotype can limit the purpose He has placed within you.

GAME PLAN FOR GROWTH

Reflection: *What labels or stereotypes have others placed on me in sports? How does 1 Samuel 16:7 remind me of God's true view of me? What would change in my life if I cared more about my heart than others' opinions?*

Challenge: This week, identify one negative label you've been carrying. Write it down, then cross it out and replace it with God's truth: *"I am His chosen, loved, and called for a higher purpose."* Each time you feel weighed down by stereotypes, remember that God looks at your heart and character, not the outward labels from others.

FAITH HUDDLE

Prayer: Dear Father, thank You for seeing my heart when the world looks only at the outside. Help me rise above the labels and stereotypes and find confidence in being Your chosen daughter. Teach me to value what You see in me above all else. **Amen.**

CHAPTER 2: PURPOSE & ALL GLORY TO GOD

6

ALL EYES ON HIM

"I keep my eyes always on the Lord. With him at my right hand, I will not be shaken."
Psalm 16:8

BEYOND THE SCOREBOARD

Lesson: Julie Ertz, a two-time World Cup champion with the U.S. Women's National Soccer Team, has played on some of the biggest stages in sports. With millions watching, the pressure could easily push her to focus on fame, performance, or proving herself. Yet Julie is widely known for openly giving God the glory after games and interviews, reminding others that her purpose is bigger than soccer. Many times she has said she plays with joy and confidence because her eyes are set on Christ, not on the crowd or the spotlight.

Psalm 16:8 reminds us, *"I keep my eyes always on the Lord. With him at my right hand, I will not be shaken."* To keep our eyes on the Lord means to focus on His presence above the distractions—above nerves, pressure, comparison, or fame. Just as a runner locks her gaze on the finish line, we are called to lock our hearts on Christ. Julie models this truth. She always competes with true passion, but redirects the spotlight back to Him. Her career proves that true success isn't measured in trophies but in glorifying God through every moment on and off the field. Julie's steadiness in soccer comes from knowing that God is with her, win or lose.

The connection between Julie and Psalm 16:8 is clear. She proves that even at the highest level, when your eyes and heart are set on the Lord, the distractions don't control you. For female athletes, this is encouragement to remember that your worth isn't measured by stats, likes, or medals. True confidence comes from focusing on God's presence. When your gaze stays on Him, nothing can shake who you are as an athlete or the purpose He's given you through your sport.

GAME PLAN FOR GROWTH

Reflection: *What distractions most often pull my focus away from God when I compete? What can I do this week to keep my focus on the Lord and redirect the spotlight back to Him instead of myself?*

Challenge: This week, before every practice or game, pause and pray Psalm 16:8: *"I keep my eyes always on the Lord. I will not be shaken."* Each time nerves or pressure creep in, remind yourself that your focus is on Christ, not on the scoreboard or other distractions. Take every opportunity to glorify Him in how you compete.

FAITH HUDDLE

Prayer: Thank You, Lord, for being with me in every moment of competition. Help me keep my eyes on You and not on the pressure or the distractions around me. Win or lose, teach me to redirect the spotlight back to You and to play with confidence that comes from Your presence. **Amen.**

7

POWERED BY PURPOSE

"And we know that in all things God works for the good of those who love him, who have been called according to his purpose."
Romans 8:28

BEYOND THE SCOREBOARD

Lesson: Maya Moore is one of the greatest basketball players in the WNBA. She was a league MVP, a four-time champion, and an Olympic gold medalist. Yet at the peak of her career, when she could have continued to chase more titles, Maya did something that shocked the world—she walked away from the game. Why? Because she believed God was calling her to a bigger purpose. She chose to step into ministry and social justice work, pouring her time into freeing an innocent man from prison and using her platform to serve Christ outside of basketball.

Romans 8:28 reminds us that God works all things for the good of those who love Him and are called according to His purpose. It means your life isn't random or wasted. God has a plan for every experience, victory, and even setback. For Maya, basketball was a gift, but it wasn't the ultimate goal. Her real calling was to glorify God by serving people and living out her faith courageously.

Maya models Romans 8:28. She shows that purpose isn't about collecting trophies but about answering God's call, even when it requires sacrifice. This is inspiring encouragement for young athletes to remember: your sport is part of your purpose, but it isn't all of it. God may use your discipline, your influence, and your struggles to impact lives in ways you can't see yet. When you trust His purpose, you are truly powered by Him.

GAME PLAN FOR GROWTH

Reflection: *What do I believe God's bigger purpose is for my life beyond sports? How can I use my platform, big or small, to glorify Him this week? When have I seen God work something for good in my life?*

Challenge: This week, write down one way you can use your sport to serve others instead of just yourself—encouraging a teammate, helping a younger player, or pointing someone to Christ. Let your actions reflect that your purpose is bigger than the game.

FAITH HUDDLE

Prayer: Thank You, Lord, for creating me with a purpose far greater than the wins or losses. Help me to see how You are working in every detail of my life. Teach me to use my gifts to and talents serve others and glorify You, just like Maya Moore. **Amen.**

8

CROWNED FOR HIS GLORY

"And when the Chief Shepherd appears, you will receive the crown of glory that will never fade away."
1 Peter 5:4

Lesson: Brianna Rollins-McNeal sprinted her way to Olympic gold in the 100-meter hurdles at the 2016 Rio Games. The world saw her speed, power, and discipline, but when she crossed the finish line, her first reaction wasn't to bask in the spotlight. She dropped to her knees on the track, lifted her hands, and declared, *"All glory to God."* For Brianna, the crown that mattered most wasn't made of gold—it was the eternal crown promised by Christ.

1 Peter 5:4 says, *"And when the Chief Shepherd appears, you will receive the crown of glory that will never fade away."* This verse is talking about Jesus, our Chief Shepherd, who will one day reward His faithful followers with a crown that lasts forever. Earthly trophies and medals are exciting, but they fade, break, or get forgotten over time. The crown from Christ is different than earthly crowns. It never fades, and it has eternal value. It reminds us

that our greatest victories aren't about applause from people but about living in a way that honors God.

Brianna's actions and beliefs are in line with the Scripture verse. Her gold medal was an incredible achievement, but her immediate response showed where her heart was anchored in Christ. She lived the truth that glory belongs to God alone. For female athletes, this is inspiration to shift your perspective: your wins and achievements are good, but they are not the ultimate prize. The greatest crown you can receive is living your life for Christ and reflecting His glory in all you do.

GAME PLAN FOR GROWTH

Reflection: *What earthly "crowns" or rewards do I chase most often in my sport? How does 1 Peter 5:4 shift my perspective on success? How can I give God glory in both my wins and losses this week?*

_____

_____

Challenge: After a practice or game, pause for a moment and ask yourself: "*Who gets the glory for this?*" Then speak a short prayer giving credit to God before posting, celebrating, or moving on. Let others see through your actions that your greatest prize is to honor Him.

FAITH HUDDLE

Prayer: God, thank You for every gift and opportunity You've given me through sports. Help me remember that the greatest crown isn't a medal or trophy, but the eternal glory You promise. Teach me to give You the credit in every victory and every struggle. **Amen.**

CHAPTER 3: HUMILITY & GRATITUDE

9

A HUMBLED HEART

"He has shown you, O mortal, what is good. And what does the Lord require of you? To act justly and to love mercy and to walk humbly with your God."
Micah 6:8

BEYOND THE SCOREBOARD

Lesson: Leah Amico is one of the most decorated softball players to play the sport—three Olympic gold medals, a College World Series champion, and a Hall of Fame career. With a resume like that, she could have easily lived in the spotlight. However, what sets Leah apart is how she chooses to walk in humility. No matter how bright the stage or how loud the praise, she constantly points people back to Christ. She once said her greatest joy wasn't the medals, but the platform God gave her to honor Him and to encourage other female athletes.

Micah 6:8 reminds us that God doesn't require fame, clout, or perfection. What He desires is a heart that acts justly, shows mercy, and walks humbly with Him. Humility doesn't mean thinking less of yourself—it means thinking of God and others more. Young athletes, this verse makes it simple and clear: honor Him in how you play, treat people fairly, and remember that your talent is a gift, not something to boast about.

Leah lived this out every time she stepped on the softball field. She celebrated her teammates, respected opponents, and refused to make the spotlight about herself. Her humility showed that greatness in sports isn't about pride—it's about character.

Leah's story is encouragement to carry a humbled heart in every part of the game. Whether you're on the bench or the big stage, your value doesn't come from applause or the spotlight. It comes from walking with God. That's what true victory looks like.

GAME PLAN FOR GROWTH

Reflection: *Where am I most tempted to make my sport about me instead of God? What does it mean to "walk humbly" with God in my daily practices or competitions? How can I celebrate others more this week instead of chasing credit for myself?*

Challenge: This week, take one action that shifts the focus away from yourself. Celebrate a teammate's success, thank your coach, or encourage an opponent. Humility is powerful—it shows others that your confidence comes from Christ, not clout.

FAITH HUDDLE

Prayer: Lord, thank You for reminding me that humility is strength, not weakness. Help me walk closely with You, act with fairness, and celebrate others above myself. Teach me to carry a humbled heart in every practice, game, and moment of life. **Amen.**

10

ADORNED WITH HUMILITY

"All of you, clothe yourselves with humility toward one another, because, 'God opposes the proud but shows favor to the humble.'"
1 Peter 5:5

BEYOND THE SCOREBOARD

Lesson: Shawn Johnson East, Olympic gold medal gymnast, knows what it's like to live under the weight of high expectations. In the 2008 Beijing Olympics, many expected her to win gold in nearly every event. Instead, she came home with three silvers and one gold. That could have crushed her confidence, but Shawn chose a different response—humility. She praised her teammates, celebrated Nastia Liukin's victories, and said she was simply proud to be part of her team's success. That's what humility looks like in action: celebrating others even when the spotlight isn't on you.

1 Peter 5:5 tells us to "clothe ourselves with humility." Just like putting on your uniform before a game, humility is something people should see in how you act. This means how you treat teammates, opponents, and even yourself when things don't go as planned. Humility isn't about thinking less of your talent; it's about remembering that your talent is a gift from God, not something to boast about.

Shawn lived this truth beyond her gymnastics. She's openly admitted her own struggles with body image and identity, reminding young athletes that medals don't equal worth. She now uses her platform to mentor and encourage other gymnasts, choosing transparency over pride. Her story shows that true greatness isn't found in medals or applause—it's found in living with humility and pointing back to Christ. This is a reminder that humility makes your witness shine brighter than any trophy.

GAME PLAN FOR GROWTH

Reflection: *How can I "clothe myself with humility" in the way I treat my teammates or opponents? Do I struggle with celebrating others when they succeed instead of me? Where can I remind myself this week that my talent is a gift, not my identity?*

Challenge: This week, choose one moment to practice humility in action by shifting the focus on someone else's success. Let humility be what people notice about you, the same way they notice your uniform.

FAITH HUDDLE

Prayer: Thank You, God, for showing me through Shawn's story that humility is strength, not weakness. Help me wear humility in every part of my life—on the field, in the gym, and with my team. Teach me to use my talent to point back to You. **Amen.**

11

KINGDOM BEFORE CLOUT

"But seek first his kingdom and his righteousness, and all these things will be given to you as well."
Matthew 6:33

BEYOND THE SCOREBOARD

Lesson: When **Sydney McLaughlin-Levrone** qualified for the USA Olympic team as a teenager in 2016, she was instantly thrown into the spotlight. By the time she broke the 400-meter hurdles world record—twice—she had become one of the most recognizable names in track and field. Fame, media attention, and endorsement deals could have easily become her focus. But instead of chasing clout, Sydney has consistently pointed back to Christ. After one of her record-breaking runs, she commented: *"Records come and go. The glory of God is eternal."*

Matthew 6:33 reminds us that we're called to seek God's Kingdom first, above all else. For teen athletes, this means resisting the temptation to measure worth by medals, trophies, or records. It means choosing God's approval over chasing headlines or attention. When we put Him first, He promises to provide what we need—peace, identity, and purpose that last longer than any championship race or podium moment.

Sydney lives this out by refusing to let the spotlight define her. Whether she's being celebrated as the best in the world or facing intense media pressure, her focus stays fixed on Christ. Her story shows that clout fades, but God's Kingdom is eternal.

This is encouragement for all female athletes to follow Sydney's lead. Your worth isn't built on popularity, trophies, or applause. True greatness comes when you choose His Kingdom over clout, living with confidence that God's plan for you is better than anything the world can offer.

GAME PLAN FOR GROWTH

Reflection: *Where am I tempted to chase attention, applause, or recognition in my sport? What does it mean for me to seek God's Kingdom first in training or competition? How can I honor God in my sport?*

Challenge: This week, after a race, practice, or workout, take one moment to redirect the spotlight back to God. Say a prayer of thanks, share an encouraging word with a teammate, or give credit to God instead of yourself. Small acts of humility train your heart to seek the Kingdom first over clout.

FAITH HUDDLE

Prayer: Heavenly Father, thank You for showing me that true success is found in seeking Your Kingdom above everything else. Help me resist the pull of trophies, medals, and applause, and instead use my gifts to bring glory to You. Teach me to keep my eyes fixed on Your Kingdom. **Amen.**

12

GRATEFUL IN ROUGH WATERS

"Give thanks in all circumstances; for this is God's will for you in Christ Jesus."
1 Thessalonians 5:18

Lesson: Bethany Hamilton is one of the most inspiring stories in sports. At just 13 years old, she was attacked by a 14-foot tiger shark while surfing in Hawaii. She lost her left arm and nearly her life, yet her response stunned the world. Instead of walking away from her sport, Bethany returned to the ocean just one month later. Within two years, she was competing again at the highest levels and has since placed among the best in the world. Her journey proves that resilience and faith can carry you through unimaginable challenges.

Bethany's story isn't only about her comeback—it's also about her gratitude. She has said: *"I might not have two arms, but I have a thankful heart, and I know God can still use me. God gave me this story for a reason."* Bethany consistently thanks God, not for the pain itself, but for how He has used her story to encourage others. She chooses to focus on what she still can do rather than on what she lost.

1 Thessalonians 5:18 calls us to give thanks in all circumstances. That doesn't mean pretending hardships don't hurt. It means trusting God enough to thank Him even in the middle of them. Gratitude becomes an anchor in the storm. Bethany's story reminds us that setbacks, losses, or injuries don't define you. Your response does. For young female athletes, gratitude shifts the focus from disappointment to opportunity, from loss to lessons, and from self to Christ.

GAME PLAN FOR GROWTH

Reflection: *What is one challenge in my life where I can thank God instead of complaining? What can I thank God for today, even if it feels small?*

_____

_____

_____

Challenge: This week, write down three things you're thankful for even during a tough season—whether it's an injury, a loss, or disappointment. Try to find the positive in the hard days. Thank God for those things and ask Him to show you how He is at work in your story.

FAITH HUDDLE

Prayer: Father, thank You for using even the hardest situations for good. Help me to choose gratitude when I feel frustrated or discouraged. Teach me to trust that You have a bigger plan for me and to let my thankfulness shine through even in rough waters. **Amen.**

YOUR VOICE MATTERS

At NextLevel Publications, we're passionate about creating meaningful resources that help female athletes grow—not just in their sport, but in their walk with Christ. Every story, scripture, challenge, and prayer was thoughtfully chosen to show how your sport and faith can work together to shape who you're becoming.

If this devotional has strengthened your faith or encouraged your game, we'd love to hear which devotion(s) have impacted you the most. Leaving a short review not only supports our faith-based mission but also helps other young athletes discover a book that could impact their lives too.

Thanks for being part of God's team! Let your voice encourage the next female athlete in building her faith and confidence. Please scan the QR code below to leave a review. Your voice truly matters.

CHAPTER 4: INTEGRITY & RESPECT

13

CHARACTER BEATS STATS

"Whoever walks in integrity walks securely, but whoever takes crooked paths will be found out."
Proverbs 10:9

Lesson: Julie Chu, a four-time Olympian for Team USA Hockey, is remembered less for her personal stats and more for her remarkable character. Competing on the world's biggest stage, she earned medals and recognition, but what teammates and opponents speak about most is her integrity. After heartbreaking Olympic defeats, Julie was seen hugging Canadian rivals with genuine respect, showing that relationships mattered more than results.

Proverbs 10:9 reminds us that integrity creates security. For athletes, this means living in a way that doesn't depend on stats or approval. Records can be broken, medals fade, but character is permanent. When you choose honesty, respect, and humility, you're walking in integrity with Christ—and that gives a confidence that no scoreboard can take away.

Julie's career proves this truth. While her stats were impressive, her legacy is built on how she treated others. Coaches, teammates, and even rivals describe her as one of the most respected players in the game. Her story teaches young female athletes that the way you carry yourself matters far more than the numbers on a scoresheet.

For you, this means remembering that your true confidence comes from Christ, not from comparison or clout. Wins and losses will come and go, but your character—rooted in faith—will always speak louder than stats.

GAME PLAN FOR GROWTH

Reflection: *What matters more to me right now—my stats or my character? How do I treat my teammates and opponents in tough moments? What steps can I take to walk with Christ's integrity?*

_____

_____

_____

Challenge: This week, choose one action that highlights your character over stats—encourage a teammate who outperforms you or congratulate an opponent. Let your actions show that integrity and character are your true wins.

FAITH HUDDLE

Prayer: Jesus, thank You for reminding me that integrity matters more than numbers. Help me focus less on stats and more on how I treat others. Teach me to walk securely in You, building character that honors Your name. **Amen.**

14

INTEGRITY IN EVERY REP

"The integrity of the upright guides them, but the unfaithful are destroyed by their duplicity."
Proverbs 11:3

BEYOND THE SCOREBOARD

Lesson: Adeline Gray is a six-time world champion wrestler and one of the most respected athletes in her sport. Wrestling demands grit, but Adeline is admired not only for her wins but also for her character. She's been outspoken about her faith in Christ and how it has shaped her choices, on and off the mat. Through victories, injuries, and tough training seasons, she has built her reputation on consistency, honesty, and respect. Her story proves that integrity isn't just about competition—it's about who you are in every step of the journey.

Proverbs 11:3 says integrity is what *guides* the upright. For athletes, this means your character directs your decisions when no one is watching—whether in training, in the locker room, or during the pressure of a big match. Stats and trophies may show what you've accomplished, but integrity reveals who you are.

Adeline embodies this verse. Coaches and teammates know that they can count on her to train hard, compete with respect, and honor Christ in how she carries herself. Her example shows that true strength on the mat isn't measured by medals—it's measured by her unwavering character. Integrity is what makes your steps secure, on the mat and in life.

GAME PLAN FOR GROWTH

Reflection: *Do I let integrity guide me in how I train and compete? What choices do I face where it's easier to cut corners than to do what's right? How can I let my character shine this week?*

_____

_____

_____

Challenge: Make one choice this week that reflects integrity, even if it's hard—finish every drill with 100% effort, admit a mistake, or show honesty in competition. Integrity in the small steps builds strength for the big ones.

FAITH HUDDLE

Prayer: Dear Lord, thank You for reminding me that integrity is my true guide in life. Help me walk in honesty and respect, both in training and competition. Teach me to value my character above trophies and to let my steps reflect Your truth. **Amen.**

15

RESPECT IN THE MOMENT

"Show proper respect to everyone, love the family of believers, fear God, honor the emperor."
1 Peter 2:17

Lesson: Brittany Lincicome has been one of the most respected golfers on the LPGA tour, not just because of her powerful swing but because of her heart for others. A two-time major champion, she has been praised for her sportsmanship, kindness to fans, and generosity toward younger players. Instead of letting her achievements make her prideful, Brittany consistently shows honor to those around her—staying after rounds to sign autographs, encouraging rookies, and congratulating competitors even when she doesn't win. Her actions prove that real respect comes from seeing others as valuable, not just yourself.

1 Peter 2:17 gives us a clear command: *"Show proper respect to everyone."* For young athletes, this doesn't stop with teammates—it extends to coaches, officials, opponents, and even fans. Respect means more than polite words; it's choosing to honor others in the way you carry yourself on and off

the course. Brittany's career reminds us that character speaks louder than trophies.

Brittany's example shows that respect isn't weakness—it's strength rooted in Christ. Wins fade, but the way you treat people is remembered forever. The call is simple: compete hard, but treat others with dignity. Respectful behavior honors God and makes your witness shine in sports.

GAME PLAN FOR GROWTH

Reflection: *Do I respect coaches, refs, and opponents as much as I respect my teammates? How can I "show respect to everyone" in my sport this week? Who can I encourage in competition instead of focusing only on myself?*

Challenge: Choose one intentional act of respect this week—thank a referee, celebrate an opponent's success, or support a struggling teammate. Respect reflects Christ more than any medal or scoreboard ever could.

FAITH HUDDLE

Prayer: God, thank You for reminding me that respect honors You as much as it honors others. Teach me to value people the way You do and to compete in a way that reflects Christ. Help my actions speak louder than my wins. **Amen.**

16

REVERENCE IN THE DETAILS

"And whatever you do, whether in word or deed, do it all in the name of the Lord Jesus, giving thanks to God the Father through him."

Colossians 3:17

BEYOND THE SCOREBOARD

Lesson: With seven Olympic medals and 25 World Championship golds, **Simone Biles** is widely regarded as the greatest gymnast of all time. What sets her at the top of her game? It's how she trains and competes—with reverence, discipline, and faith. She acknowledges her abilities are a gift from God, and she doesn't perform to impress the crowd. Instead, she competes to honor her Creator.

In training, Simone is known for being meticulous, focused, and fully present. She listens, encourages others, and honors the hard work behind every small detail. She prays before events, thanks God after each meet, and has never lost sight of where her talent came from. At the 2021 Tokyo Olympics, Simone made headlines when she withdrew from multiple events to protect her mental health. This was hard for the world to understand. But behind that bold move was something more profound: a reverence for what God values most—her soul over her score. She reminded the world, *"God is bigger than gymnastics."*

Reverence means showing deep respect, awe, and honor, especially toward God. Colossians 3:17 reminds us that every word and deed should be done in Jesus' name, with gratitude and reverence. That includes training reps, warm-ups, stretches, and big performances. It's showing up with focus and giving your best to worship God with your effort. Simone teaches young female athletes that true greatness doesn't come from medals, but from doing every rep with integrity, thankfulness, and reverence for the One who gave you the talent. Reverence is a mindset that can shape your practice, your sportsmanship, and your attitude.

GAME PLAN FOR GROWTH

Reflection: *Do I train with gratitude, focus, and reverence, or just to "get through it"? How can I treat every rep like an act of worship?*

Challenge: This week, show reverence in how you prepare. Don't just go through the motions. Be fully present in warm-ups and pray before drills. Train like your effort is an offering to God.

FAITH HUDDLE

Prayer: Dear Jesus, thank You for the gifts You've given me. Help me show reverence in every rep and treat each moment as worship. Let my words, effort, and attitude reflect Your name. **Amen.**

SECTION II: DISCIPLINE & PERSONAL GROWTH

(WEEKS 17 - 35)

Greatness isn't given—it's forged through daily discipline, mental grit, and faith-fueled perseverance. This set of devotions equips young athletes to embrace the grind—developing habits of discipline, patience, mental toughness, and focus that fuel long-term success. Through stories of resilience and training with purpose, you will learn how to push through adversity with a Christ-centered mindset. These devotions will help you grow not just in skill, but in character, focus, and spiritual maturity.

CHAPTER 5: DISCIPLINE & TRAINING

17

HABITS THAT HONOR HIM

"Everyone who competes in the games goes into strict training. They do it to get a crown that will not last, but we do it to get a crown that will last forever."
1 Corinthians 9:25

BEYOND THE SCOREBOARD

Lesson: Gabrielle Reece, one of the most recognizable names in women's volleyball, is remembered not only for her dominance on the court but also for her consistent daily discipline. From early in her career, she embraced steady training routines—strength work, recovery, nutrition, and rest—that allowed her to perform at an elite level for years. But what made Gabrielle stand out was that her discipline extended beyond sports. She prioritized faith, family, and balance, showing that habits honoring God reach into every part of life.

1 Corinthians 9:25 reminds us that athletes train hard for crowns and trophies that eventually fade, but those who honor God with their habits are pursuing something eternal. For Gabrielle, greatness wasn't measured by her wins, but by how she stewarded her gifts. She modeled respect for her teammates, care for her body, and intentional routines that reflected God's design for discipline.

Gabrielle's example challenges female athletes to see that habits aren't just about wins—they're about worship. Every choice matters: prayer before practice, focus in drills, encouraging words to teammates. When your routines are rooted in Christ, the unseen daily work becomes a platform to glorify Him. Habits shape character, and character reveals who you're truly living for.

GAME PLAN FOR GROWTH

Reflection: *Do my daily habits reflect my faith in God? What is one habit I can improve to honor Him more consistently? How can I turn everyday routines into acts of worship?*

Challenge: This week, identify one small habit—prayer before practice, gratitude during workouts, or encouraging a teammate—and commit to it daily. Let your consistency become an offering of worship to God.

FAITH HUDDLE

Prayer: Heavenly Father, thank You for reminding me that habits shape who I become. Help me create routines that honor You in training, school, and life. Teach me to glorify You not only in big moments but in the daily choices that build character. **Amen.**

18

OBEDIENCE DRIVES GREATNESS

"Let us fix our eyes on Jesus, the author and perfecter of our faith."
"Anyone who loves me will obey my teaching. My Father will love them,
and we will come to them and make our home with them."
John 14:23

BEYOND THE SCOREBOARD

Lesson: Claire Wolford, a collegiate cheerleader and outspoken Christian, models what it looks like when love for Christ becomes daily obedience. Cheer and dance demand strict training—hours of drills, strength work, timing, and trust—but Claire's discipline doesn't stop at the gym. She frames her routines around God's Word: praying before practice, speaking life to teammates, honoring coaches' decisions, and guarding what she posts online. She chooses recovery over late-night distractions, encourages teammates who miss landings, and keeps her words clean even when pressure spikes. Her habits reflect a heart that wants to please God more than impress a crowd, and that steady obedience shapes every performance.

John 14:23 teaches that obedience flows from love. We don't obey to earn God's approval; we obey because we belong to Him. For athletes, that means letting Scripture direct the little decisions—how you train, compete, rest, and respond when plans shift. Obedience is choosing God's way when emotions run loud: telling the truth, owning mistakes, resisting gossip, and showing respect even when a routine or play gets reworked.

Claire's example reminds us that greatness isn't just a performance night; it's the pattern of faithfulness you stack one choice at a time. When your habits are shaped by Scripture, your talent becomes a testimony. For female athletes, this is your edge: train your body with discipline and your heart with obedience. That's where real greatness grows, and that's how your sport becomes worship.

GAME PLAN FOR GROWTH

Reflection: *Do my choices show obedience to Christ even when no one is watching? What small area of my life needs more discipline and faithfulness? How can my love for God guide my obedience this week?*

Challenge: Pick one daily action—social media use, attitude at practice, or time in prayer—and commit to obeying God in that area. Obedience in small things builds greatness that honors Christ.

FAITH HUDDLE

Prayer: God, thank You for showing me that greatness comes through obedience to You. Help me choose Your ways in my training, words, and actions. Teach me to love You so deeply that obedience becomes my first response. **Amen.**

19

FOCUS FUELED DISCIPLINE

"Set your minds on things above, not on earthly things."
Colossians 3:2

BEYOND THE SCOREBOARD

Lesson: Dara Torres is one of the most decorated female swimmers in Olympic history, competing in five different Games across 24 years. What set her apart wasn't just her speed but her focus. Training through injuries, setbacks, and even motherhood, Dara showed the world that discipline comes from keeping your eyes fixed on what matters most. She famously returned to Olympic competition at age 41, proving that when you fuel discipline with focus, you can break barriers others think are impossible.

Colossians 3:2 reminds us to set our minds on "things above." In sports this means fixing your focus not just on medals or records, but on God's purpose in your life. Discipline without focus becomes an empty routine. But discipline fueled by the right focus—Christ—turns your training into worship. Dara's success didn't come from talent alone; it was built on countless early mornings, strict habits, and a mindset that refused to drift.

Her story challenges young athletes to ask: *Where is my focus?* Is it on comparison, pressure, or perfection—or on honoring God through daily choices? Dara's career proves that focus creates discipline, and discipline shapes greatness. When your mind is set on Christ, your training gains eternal value. Every lap, sprint, or rep becomes more than preparation—it becomes a testimony of faith in action.

GAME PLAN FOR GROWTH

Reflection: *Where do I lose focus most often—competition, school, or social media? How can I redirect that focus toward Christ this week? What habits in my training need more consistency?*

Challenge: This week, choose one area of training where you've been distracted. Commit to staying consistent and prayerful in that space, focusing on Christ as your reason for discipline.

FAITH HUDDLE

Prayer: Father, I'm grateful for the focus and discipline You instill in me through sports. Teach me to set my mind on things above, not on distractions that pull me away from You. Strengthen my routines and my heart so that every effort brings glory to Your name. **Amen.**

20

POWERED BY PRAYER

"Devote yourselves to prayer, being watchful and thankful."
Colossians 4:2

BEYOND THE SCOREBOARD

Lesson: Before the first whistle blows or the scoreboard lights up, Baylor University's women's volleyball team is already setting the tone—on their knees. Freshman standout **Kendal Murphy** has shared that prayer isn't just a side note for the Bears, it's their foundation. "Putting God at the center of everything...remembering who we're playing for," she explained. That conviction shows up in how the team approaches every match.

At Baylor, prayer is woven into their culture. Before each game, Kendal and her teammates gather in a circle on the court, praying for God's guidance, thanking Him for the chance to compete, and even lifting up their opponents. Afterward, whether in victory or defeat, they pray again—offering gratitude and grace. Their consistency proves prayer isn't a superstition; it's a discipline that keeps their hearts grounded.

Colossians 4:2 calls us to "devote" ourselves to prayer—meaning to treat it like fuel, not an afterthought. For Kendal and her teammates, prayer sharpens focus, calms nerves, and keeps their identity anchored in Christ instead of the scoreboard. Their example shows that prayer belongs in every arena, not just in quiet moments at night.

For young female athletes, this is a reminder: when prayer drives your game, you're powered by more than skill—you're fueled by God Himself.

GAME PLAN FOR GROWTH

Reflection: *How often do I invite God into my sport? Do I pray only when I feel pressure, or consistently like Kendal's team? What's one way I can bring prayer into my training this week?*

Challenge: Before your next practice or competition, pause to pray—even if it's just 30 seconds. Thank God for the opportunity, ask Him for focus, and pray for teammates and opponents.

FAITH HUDDLE

Prayer: Lord, I give thanks for the reminder that prayer fuels both my heart and my performance. Teach me to stay disciplined in prayer, inviting You into every practice, game, and moment. May my sport always reflect Your power. **Amen.**

CHAPTER 6: PATIENCE & PERSEVERANCE

21

FAITH THAT FUELS THE CLIMB

"For we live by faith, not by sight."
2 Corinthians 5:7

Lesson: Chaunté Lowe, a four-time Olympian and American record–holding high jumper, faced a mountain no training could prepare her for: breast cancer. At the height of her career, with dreams of another Olympics ahead, she was forced into a fight for her life. Chemo treatments left her weak, uncertain if she'd ever return to competition. But Chaunté chose to trust God even when she couldn't see the way forward.

She shared openly that her faith was her anchor. Instead of letting fear control her, she leaned on prayer, Scripture, and the belief that God had a purpose bigger than medals. She trained during chemo, refusing to give up, and later returned to competition as a testimony of God's strength in weakness.

2 Corinthians 5:7 tells us to "live by faith, not by sight." This means trusting God when the results, stats, or circumstances don't look promising.

Chaunté embodied this truth, showing that faith fuels perseverance when sight gives you every reason to quit.

Chaunté's story reminds young female athletes that uncertainty is part of life, but faith keeps you climbing. Whether you're battling injury, setbacks, or doubts, remember: your faith in Christ is what gives you the courage to keep pressing on.

GAME PLAN FOR GROWTH

Reflection: *When has life felt uncertain for me? Do I let fear stop me, or do I trust God to guide me? What's one area of my sport I need to give fully to Him?*

Challenge: This week, memorize 2 Corinthians 5:7. Whenever discouragement or fear creeps in, repeat it to yourself as a declaration of faith.

FAITH HUDDLE

Prayer: Jesus, thank You for being my anchor when life feels uncertain. Teach me to trust You when I can't see the outcome and to let my faith fuel perseverance in sports and life. **Amen.**

22

TOUGH, TESTED & TRIUMPHANT

"Blessed is the one who perseveres under trial because, having stood the test, that person will receive the crown of life that the Lord has promised to those who love him."

James 1:12

BEYOND THE SCOREBOARD

Lesson: Helen Maroulis made history in 2016 when she became the first American woman to win Olympic gold in wrestling. But her journey wasn't only about victory—it was about what came after. Following her triumph, Helen faced repeated concussions, anxiety, and depression that nearly forced her to retire. Doctors told her to give up the sport she loved. She felt broken, sidelined, and uncertain if she'd ever step on the mat again.

Instead of quitting, Helen leaned on her faith. She sought God's strength in prayer and clung to the truth that her worth wasn't tied to medals. Slowly, she rebuilt—body, mind, and spirit. Against the odds, she returned to compete internationally, proving that perseverance through trials creates deeper strength than any trophy can show.

James 1:12 promises that those who persevere under trial will receive the "crown of life." For female athletes, this means the battles you face—injury, bench time, or setbacks—are opportunities to trust God and grow stronger in Him. Helen's resilience shows that triumph isn't about never falling; it's about rising again with faith fueling each step.

Her story challenges young athletes to embrace trials as part of the journey. When you remain faithful through hard times, your victory goes beyond the scoreboard—it becomes eternal.

GAME PLAN FOR GROWTH

Reflection: *What trials am I facing in my sport right now? How can I trust God to strengthen me in the middle of them?*

_____

_____

_____

Challenge: This week, when a challenge comes—whether it's a tough practice, bench time, or injury—pause and pray James 1:12. Ask God to use the test to build perseverance in you.

FAITH HUDDLE

Prayer: Heavenly Father, I give thanks for the trials that shape me into who You've called me to be. Help me stay faithful when life feels heavy and give me the courage to persevere with strength rooted in You. May every triumph reflect Your glory. **Amen.**

23

PERSEVERE FOR HIS PROMISE

"You need to persevere so that when you have done the will of God, you will receive what he has promised."
Hebrews 10:36

Lesson: As a child, **Stacy Lewis** dreamed of playing golf at the highest level. But at age 11, doctors diagnosed her with scoliosis, a spine condition that threatened to end her athletic journey. She wore a back brace for seven years, 23 hours a day, while other kids enjoyed a normal life. Even after major back surgery, her future in golf was uncertain. Many doubted if she would ever compete at a high level.

But Stacy didn't let the setback stop her. She chose perseverance. Through countless hours of rehab and disciplined practice, she eventually earned a spot on the University of Arkansas team, then climbed all the way to become the world's #1 female golfer and a two-time major champion. Stacy has openly credited God's faithfulness for giving her the strength to press on through the difficult times.

Hebrews 10:36 tells us perseverance is required to see God's promises fulfilled. For you as an athlete, this means pushing through seasons of injury, self-doubt, or setbacks—trusting God's bigger plan. Stacy's story shows that perseverance isn't just about grit; it's about faith in God's promise that He is with you, even when the climb is steep.

The Scripture tell us that perseverance through struggle grows lasting character. When you keep pressing on with Christ, the reward is greater than medals—it's the strength of faith formed in the journey.

GAME PLAN FOR GROWTH

Reflection: *What trial in my sport is testing my perseverance right now? How can I trust God's promise even when the outcome looks uncertain? Where do I need to keep pressing forward in faith?*

Challenge: This week, when you face frustration or fatigue, pause and pray Hebrews 10:36. Ask God to give you the strength to keep going and the faith to trust His promises.

FAITH HUDDLE

Prayer: Heavenly Father, I'm grateful for the reminder that perseverance grows my faith. Help me stay steady when challenges feel overwhelming and give me courage to trust Your promises. May my perseverance point others to You. **Amen.**

24

TRUST, THE HARVEST AWAITS

Let us not become weary in doing good, for at the proper time we will reap a harvest if we do not give up."
Galatians 6:9

BEYOND THE SCOREBOARD

Lesson: Trusting God's promise means believing even when you can't yet see the results. **Carli Lloyd,** one of the most respected players in U.S. Women's National Team history, lived this out. After the high of winning Olympic gold in 2008, her career hit a wall—knee injuries, inconsistent play, and the doubt of critics weighed heavily on her. She could have quit. Instead, Carli chose to trust God's timing.

She committed herself to extra training sessions, intentional rehab, and steady prayer. She leaned on her faith to carry her through the quiet, unseen seasons when the spotlight wasn't shining. Then came her breakthrough in the 2015 Women's World Cup final. Carli stunned the world with a historic hat trick, two goals from midfield, and the Golden Ball award. That night wasn't luck—it was the harvest of years of perseverance, preparation, and faith in God's plan.

Galatians 6:9 reminds us not to grow weary when the waiting feels long. Like Carli, you may not see the reward right away, but God is growing something through every rep, every practice, and every prayer. The harvest may not be instant, but it's certain. Your role is to stay faithful in the unseen, trusting His timing.

GAME PLAN FOR GROWTH

Reflection: *What "hidden work" in my training or faith journey feels tiring right now? How can I trust that God is preparing a harvest I can't see yet? What promises from His Word give me the strength to keep going?*

FAITH HUDDLE

Prayer: Father, I'm thankful that every seed I plant in faith matters to You. Teach me to keep working with patience, even when the results don't come quickly. Help me trust Your timing and believe that the harvest is soon ahead. **Amen.**

CHAPTER 7: RESILIENCE & RECOVERY

25

BOUNCE BACK BELIEF

"But those who hope in the Lord will renew their strength. They will soar on wings like eagles; they will run and not grow weary, they will walk and not be faint."
Isaiah 40:31

Lesson: Dana Vollmer knows what it means to bounce back. As a young swimmer, she was diagnosed with a heart condition that put her future in doubt. Later, injuries and setbacks forced breaks from the pool. She also stepped away to become a mom before attempting a comeback many thought impossible. Through uncertainty and slow rebuilds, Dana chose disciplined routines, wise rest, and a steady mindset. She kept showing up—early alarms, careful nutrition, relentless drills—believing the hidden work would matter on race day.

Isaiah 40:31 says those who hope in the Lord will renew their strength. For athletes, hope isn't wishful thinking. It's trusting God while you do the work. Waiting on the Lord looks like patient training, honest recovery, and courage to start again after disappointment. It means rooting your identity in Christ, not in times, rankings, or headlines. When your heart leans on Him, He supplies endurance your body alone can't produce.

Anchored by disciplined habits and a humble perspective, Dana returned to the world stage and excelled again. As an athlete, your road may include injuries, roster cuts, or slow progress, but hope and faith in Jesus fuels the bounce back. Keep your eyes up, do the small things well, and trust the One who renews strength. In His timing, you'll rise—steadier, stronger, and ready for the next comeback.

GAME PLAN FOR GROWTH

Reflection: *Where do I need God to renew my strength right now? How can I place my hope in Him when I feel like giving up? What setback in my sport could become part of my comeback?*

Challenge: This week, pair every tough workout or discouraging moment with a quick Isaiah 40:31 prayer. Then act: finish the rep, complete the drill, or start rehab steps. Let hope and faith in Christ Jesus fuel your next move.

FAITH HUDDLE

Prayer: Jesus, I thank You for renewing my strength when setbacks slow me down. Teach me to wait on You, train with patience, and trust Your perfect timing. Make my comeback reflect Your power and purpose. **Amen.**

26

RISE IN RESILIENCE

"We also glory in our sufferings, because we know that suffering produces perseverance; perseverance, character; and character, hope."
Romans 5:3–4

BEYOND THE SCOREBOARD

Lesson: Kayla Harrison is one of the toughest athletes in the world. A two-time Olympic gold medalist in judo, her path to greatness was marked by pain no child should endure. She survived years of abuse before finding healing through faith, supportive mentors, and the discipline of her sport. What could have destroyed her instead became the soil where resilience took root. Kayla learned that victory isn't only about medals—it's about refusing to let hardships define you.

Her comeback required more than talent. After the trauma, Kayla rebuilt herself through relentless training, therapy, and a daily decision to rise again. She leaned on God's truth and chose perseverance when the road was dark. Every grueling practice, every doubt, every moment of pain became an opportunity to grow stronger. Later in her career, she used her platform to speak boldly about overcoming hardships, encouraging others to find hope through Christ in the middle of brokenness.

Romans 5:3–4 explains that suffering produces perseverance, which shapes character and gives hope. This verse tell us that trials—injuries, pressure, criticism—aren't wasted. They shape you into someone deeper, stronger, and more faithful. Kayla's story shows that resilience doesn't mean avoiding hardship; it means rising through it, trusting God's greater plan.

Your struggles may look different, but the message is the same: with Christ, you can rise in resilience and discover hope that lasts beyond the game.

GAME PLAN FOR GROWTH

Reflection: *What struggle in my sport has tested me the most? How can I choose perseverance instead of giving up? Where have I seen God build character through my trials?*

Challenge: This week, write down one trial you're facing. Pray Romans 5:3–4 over it daily, asking God to use the struggle to grow your perseverance, character, and hope.

FAITH HUDDLE

Prayer: God, thank You for turning hardships into opportunities for growth. Help me to rise up in resilience, trusting that You are shaping my character and filling me with lasting hope. **Amen.**

27

RECOVER, RESTORE & REBUILD

"And the God of all grace, who called you to his eternal glory in Christ, after you have suffered a little while, will himself restore you and make you strong, firm and steadfast."
1 Peter 5:10

Lesson: Monique Lamoureux knows the weight of disappointment. Before earning Olympic gold with the U.S. Women's Hockey Team, she lived through years of heartbreak—silver medals, overtime losses, and constant questions about whether she and her teammates could finish the job. Each setback could have broken her confidence. Instead, Monique chose to recover, trust God's timing, and commit to rebuilding stronger than before.

Her perseverance shined in the 2018 Winter Olympics. In the final against Canada, Monique scored the tying goal late in regulation, then delivered the decisive shootout goal that clinched Team USA's first hockey gold in 20 years. What once looked like failure after failure became the foundation for triumph.

1 Peter 5:10 promises that God restores and strengthens us after hardships. As an athlete, this means injuries, bench time, or disappointing seasons are not the end of the story. Recovery isn't just physical—it's mental and spiritual. It's trusting that God can rebuild you when the weight of defeat feels overwhelming.

Monique's story proves that resilience is forged in valleys. With Christ, every setback can shape you into someone stronger, steadier, and ready for the next test. Your toughest seasons may be where God builds your strongest faith.

GAME PLAN FOR GROWTH

Reflection: *What past setback still feels heavy to me? How might God be using it to rebuild me?*

Challenge: Think of one past failure. This week, thank God for how He might be using it to grow you. Then take one step forward—whether extra effort in training or prayer—to recover, restore, and rebuild with His strength.

FAITH HUDDLE

Prayer: Father, thank You for restoring me when I feel broken. Help me recover with faith, rebuild with perseverance, and grow stronger through You. Make my heart firm and steadfast in every trial. **Amen.**

28

THE CHAMPION WITHIN

"The Lord does not look at the things people look at. People look at the outward appearance, but the Lord looks at the heart."
1 Samuel 16:7

Lesson: Candace Parker has faced challenges that could have defined her—injuries that sidelined seasons, critics who questioned her leadership, and the pressure of carrying a franchise while navigating motherhood. Yet what makes her story compelling isn't just titles or MVPs; it's the quiet choices that formed her character. She rehabbed patiently, accepted new roles, mentored younger teammates, and kept showing up with humility when the spotlight moved on. In locker rooms and huddles, she set a tone for the team: compete hard, honor people, and let your actions speak.

1 Samuel 16:7 says God does not look at outward appearance but at the heart. For athletes, that redefines greatness. It's not the headlines, highlight clips, or rankings; it's the unseen habits—how you practice, listen, apologize, and celebrate others. When the Lord weighs the heart, He values integrity over image and faithfulness over flair. Playing from the inside out means letting Him shape your mindset, words, and work ethic.

Candace's story embodies that truth. Her career has included comeback seasons, position changes, and sacrificial leadership for team success. She proved that the "champion within" grows when you root your identity in Christ more than applause. Young female athletes can do the same: train hard, tell the truth, serve your team, and keep your heart aligned with Jesus. Wins will fade, but the woman you become will not. Guard your heart, and your game will follow. That is where lasting strength is forged.

GAME PLAN FOR GROWTH

Reflection: *What do I rely on most for my confidence—appearance, stats, or heart? How can I focus more on my character than on my performance?*

Challenge: This week, shift your focus from performance to character. Encourage a teammate, practice honesty, or show humility. Let your heart, not the scoreboard, be the way you define success.

FAITH HUDDLE

Prayer: Lord, I thank You for seeing my heart even when the world looks at appearances. Teach me to value character over accolades and to live with the confidence of a true champion within. **Amen.**

CHAPTER 8:
COMMITMENT & MENTAL TOUGHNESS

29

COMMITTED IN CHRIST

"Commit to the Lord whatever you do, and he will establish your plans."
Proverbs 16:3

BEYOND THE SCOREBOARD

Lesson: Maria Fassi has become one of the most recognizable names in women's golf—not just for her long drives, but for the way she anchors her life in Christ. The LPGA standout from Mexico blends strength, discipline, and a faith-filled focus that sets her apart on and off the course.

Behind her athletic skill is a lifestyle of consistency. Maria trains six days a week, logging heavy lifts like squats, deadlifts, and lunges to build explosive power. Twice-a-day sessions in the gym sharpen her strength, while yoga and Pilates give her balance, flexibility, and mental toughness. Her commitment to her craft is impressive, but her commitment to the Lord is what truly defines her.

From her college years to her rise in the pros, Maria has been vocal about playing for something bigger than herself. She often says her career is meant to be a testimony—not only to her hard work, but to the God she serves. She carries her Bible with her on the road and turns to prayer before tournaments, asking for peace and focus no matter what the leaderboard says.

Proverbs 16:3 reminds us that when we place every practice, game, and goal in God's hands, He shapes not just our results but our character. Maria models this truth: whether she's lifting in the gym or teeing off in front of thousands, she plays with confidence because she's already surrendered the outcome to Him.

GAME PLAN FOR GROWTH

Reflection: *What part of your daily training or game do you find hard to fully commit to? How would surrendering that area to God bring you peace or purpose?*

_____

_____

_____

Challenge: This week, choose one part of your routine—stretching, conditioning, or skill drills—and intentionally dedicate it to God. Stay consistent each day, reminding yourself that every rep is an offering to Him.

FAITH HUDDLE

Prayer: God, thank You for giving me the chance to glorify You through my sport. Teach me to commit every practice and performance to You, trusting You with both the process and the results. **Amen.**

30

UNSHAKABLE SPIRIT

"We are hard pressed on every side, but not crushed; perplexed, but not in despair; persecuted, but not abandoned; struck down, but not destroyed."
2 Corinthians 4:8–9

BEYOND THE SCOREBOARD

Lesson: Jessica Long's story is one of resilience anchored in Christ. Born without fibulas, ankles, or heels, she was adopted from a Siberian orphanage and endured more than 25 surgeries before turning 18. Most would have seen these challenges as limits—but Jessica chose to see them as opportunities to glorify God.

Today, she is one of the most decorated Paralympic swimmers in history, with over 20 medals to her name. Yet what sets her apart isn't just her dominance in the pool—it's her testimony of faith. Jessica has said many times, *"My identity is not found in winning medals. It's found in who I am in Jesus."* Behind the victories are years of battling self-doubt, bullying, and body image struggles. Instead of letting those wounds define her, Jessica leaned on prayer and Scripture to remind herself of God's purpose for her life.

2 Corinthians 4:8–9 shows us that faith doesn't mean life will be easy. It means that even when trials press in from every side, we are never abandoned. Jessica embodies this truth: though life struck her with physical challenges, she was never destroyed because her spirit was grounded in Christ. Young athletes, her example reminds us that toughness isn't just physical—it's spiritual. True strength is found in trusting God to carry you when everything else feels too heavy.

GAME PLAN FOR GROWTH

Reflection: *Where do you feel the most pressure or setback in your sport right now? How can you lean on God's strength instead of your own in that area?*

Challenge: This week, when you face a tough practice, injury, or a disappointing loss, speak God's truth to yourself: *"I may be pressed, but I am not crushed. My spirit is unshakable in Christ."* Write that verse on a card and keep it in your gym bag for reference.

FAITH HUDDLE

Prayer: Lord, thank You for reminding me that no setback can destroy the spirit You've placed within me. Help me face challenges with courage, leaning on Your strength, and trusting that in You I am never defeated. **Amen.**

31

GRIT WITH GRACE

"But he said to me, 'My grace is sufficient for you, for my power is made perfect in weakness.' Therefore I will boast all the more gladly about my weaknesses, so that Christ's power may rest on me."

2 Corinthians 12:9

Lesson: Few athletes have embodied grit like skier **Lindsey Vonn**. Known as one of the greatest alpine skiers in history, she faced countless injuries—torn ligaments, concussions, fractures, and surgeries—that would have ended most careers. Yet Lindsey kept getting back up, refusing to let injuries and setbacks define her. What set her apart wasn't just her relentless comeback. It was the grace she carried through it all. She once said, *"Skiing is not just about winning, it's about pushing your limits and handling the obstacles with strength and grace."*

2 Corinthians 12:9 reminds us that God's power is made perfect in our weakness. For young female athletes, this truth can feel freeing: you don't have to be flawless. In fact, it's often in your struggles that God's strength shines the brightest. Lindsey's story shows us that grit isn't about never falling—it's about getting back up each time with determination, and doing so with grace, humility, and perseverance.

As a female athlete, you will face setbacks—injuries, tough losses, self-doubts, or criticism. But God's Word promises that His grace is enough to carry you through. Like Lindsey, you can embrace grit while relying on Christ to supply the strength you lack. As you do, you'll reflect His power more than your own. That's true grit—with God's grace.

GAME PLAN FOR GROWTH

Reflection: *Where do I need grit in my sport right now? How can I rely on God's grace instead of my own strength? When was the last time I saw God use my weakness for His purpose?*

Challenge: This week, write down one area where you feel weak—physically, mentally, or spiritually. Pray over it daily, asking God to turn your weakness into strength. Face your practices or games with grit, but let His grace guide your response.

FAITH HUDDLE

Prayer: Dear Lord, thank You for showing me that true strength is found in You. Teach me to rise after setbacks with grit and to respond gracefully. Help me rely on Your power in every challenge I face. **Amen.**

CHAPTER 9: FEARLESS & FOCUSED

32

FAITH OVER FEAR

"I sought the Lord, and he answered me; he delivered me from all my fears."

Psalm 34:4

BEYOND THE SCOREBOARD

Lesson: In the high-stakes world of Olympic softball, the pressure to be perfect can crush even the strongest player. For **Ali Aguilar**, fear of failure once shaped her entire identity. She felt her worth rise and fall with her batting average or whether she made an error on the field. *"I used to think if I made a mistake, I was a failure,"* Ali admitted, reflecting on the inner war between expectation and freedom.

But God was writing a different story. Instead of allowing mistakes to define her, Ali learned to surrender them to Christ. Games where she struck out or missed a play became opportunities to lean on grace. She discovered her value wasn't tied to flawless performance but anchored in the unshakable truth of God's love.

Psalm 34:4 promises that when we seek the Lord, He delivers us from our fears. For Ali, this meant no longer letting the replay reel of her mistakes play on repeat in her mind. By seeking God first, she could release the fear of failure and step onto the field with confidence and freedom.

As a young athlete, you may worry about letting teammates down or messing up in big moments. But faith over fear means trusting that God has already delivered you from your fears. With Him, your worth is secure, and your failures don't define you.

GAME PLAN FOR GROWTH

Reflection: *When I make a mistake, do I replay it over and over, or release it to God? What fear is God asking me to surrender to Him this week?*

Challenge: When you go about your week and you make a mistake, pause and pray Psalm 34:4. Say aloud, *"God has delivered me from fear."* Then step back into the game with confidence and courage.

FAITH HUDDLE

Prayer: Father, thank You for delivering me from my fear of messing up or letting my teammates down. Help me to release the mistakes that I hold onto and remember that my worth is secure in You. Give me courage to play freely and fearlessly. **Amen.**

33

CALM UNDER PRESSURE

"You will keep in perfect peace those whose minds are steadfast, because they trust in you."
Isaiah 26:3

BEYOND THE SCOREBOARD

Lesson: Sloane Stephens knows what it feels like when pressure tightens your chest. After a year derailed by a stress fracture in her foot, she returned to win the 2017 US Open, staying composed point by point on one of tennis's loudest stages. In big moments she leans on her routine—takes a deep breath, bounces the ball, and commits to the next swing. Sloane refuses to let the score control her. *"I've been in a place where it's been dark and it's been deep and it's been sad ... I needed to lean on my faith in God to help get me out of that dark place."*

Isaiah 26:3 promises perfect peace to the one whose mind is steadfast, because she trusts in God. For athletes, that means calm isn't an accident; it's the byproduct of an attention fixed on Him. When nerves spike, steadiness grows through small choices: a Scripture whispered between points, a reset breath, eyes up, shoulders down. Trusting in God shifts your focus from worst-case "what-ifs" to the One who holds you up, whatever the outcome.

Sloane models that mindset under pressure. Her composure isn't passive—it's a fierce, practiced focus that channels energy into the present point. You can do the same. When fear and anxiety of the moment shows up, set your mind on Christ, use your routine, and trust your abilities. Let God quiet the noise in your head so your training shows. Pressure will visit, but it doesn't have to rule you or your performance. Fix your thoughts, play the point in front of you, and let His peace guard your heart and your game.

GAME PLAN FOR GROWTH

Reflection: *What moments trigger my performance anxiety the most? Which reset—breath, verse, or routine—will I practice between points this week? How can I keep my focus on Christ when the pressure rises?*

Challenge: All week, **pair a reset routine** (deep breath + short verse) before every serve, shot, swing, or rep. Say, *"Mind on Christ, play the next point,"* and step forward with steady eyes and heart.

FAITH HUDDLE

Prayer: God, thank You for the perfect peace that steadies me under pressure. Teach me to fix my mind on You, breathe, reset, and compete with trust in my abilities instead of fear. Guard my heart and my focus today. **Amen.**

34

STRONGER THAN THE BLOCKS

"For God has not given us a spirit of fear, but of power and of love and of a sound mind."
2 Timothy 1:7

BEYOND THE SCOREBOARD

Lesson: Olympic gymnast **Laurie Hernandez** is known for her radiant smile and fearless performances, but even she has faced battles with mental blocks and anxiety. After the thrill of winning gold in Rio at just 16, she later stepped back from competition to face challenges that weren't physical—they were mental. The pressure to be perfect, the weight of expectations, and fear of mistakes created walls in her mind that no amount of practice alone could break.

Laurie has spoken openly about relying on her faith in those seasons. *"At the end of the day, medals aren't everything. My identity is in Christ,"* she said. That truth gave her the strength to recover, reset, and face the routines that once felt impossible. By clinging to God's Word, she learned to replace fear with peace and the mental blocks with trust in the Lord.

2 Timothy 1:7 reminds us that fear doesn't come from God. Instead, He gives us power, love, and self-control to over come our fears. Mental blocks may whisper "you can't," but God declares "you can." Laurie's courage proves that breaking through the mental blocks isn't about sheer willpower—it's about trusting God to calm your mind and steady your heart.

Like Laurie, you can overcome mental blocks by fixing your focus on Him. Fear may rise, but God's power within you is stronger.

GAME PLAN FOR GROWTH

Reflection: *Where do I face mental blocks in my sport? How can I invite God's Spirit to replace my fears with confidence?*

Challenge: This week, when you face a mental block—whether in practice or competition—pause and repeat 2 Timothy 1:7. Replace "fear" with "power" in your thoughts, then move forward with confidence in Christ.

FAITH HUDDLE

Prayer: God, thank You for giving me a spirit of power and love. When I feel blocked or afraid, remind me to lean on You. Help me move forward with courage and confidence in Your strength. **Amen.**

35

FOCUSED TO THE FINISH

"No discipline seems pleasant at the time, but painful. Later on, however, it produces a harvest of righteousness and peace for those who have been trained by it."
Hebrews 12:11

BEYOND THE SCOREBOARD

Lesson: Kendall Coyne Schofield, captain of the U.S. Women's Hockey Team, is known for her blazing speed on the ice. She stunned the sports world when she competed in the NHL All-Star Skills Competition, proving she could keep pace with the fastest men in the game. But behind that spotlight moment lies years of relentless training, discipline, and a focused faith that keeps her grounded.

Growing up, Kendall was often the smallest player on the ice, but she refused to let size stop her. She trained longer, skated harder, and developed a toughness that carried her to an Olympic gold. She's spoken about her faith giving her perspective, reminding her that her platform isn't just about hockey—it's about honoring God in how she competes and leads others.

Hebrews 12:11 reminds us that discipline isn't easy—it takes sacrifice, sweat, focus, and pain—but it leads to growth and success. Kendall's life proves this. Her intense focus in practice, leadership in the locker room, and perseverance through challenges show that true greatness is built long before game day. As an athlete, her example of focus is clear: discipline is not just about perfect drills—it's about staying committed to the habits, character, and focusing on a faith that shape you for life.

GAME PLAN FOR GROWTH

Reflection: *Where do I need more discipline in my training or faith? How can I see discipline as God shaping me for growth instead of holding me back?*

Challenge: This week, identify one small habit you can commit to daily—extra reps, stretching, or prayer before practice. Stick with it, knowing God uses discipline to strengthen both body and soul.

FAITH HUDDLE

Prayer: God, thank You for shaping me through discipline. Help me stay focused and committed, even when it's hard. Let my training honor You, and may my habits build both strength and faith. **Amen.**

SECTION III: TEAM VALUES & IMPACT

(WEEKS 36 - 45)

The most memorable teams aren't just made up of stars—they're built on a sisterhood of trust, humility, unity, and a shared purpose. This section of devotions teaches young female athletes how to lead with influence, serve with humility, lift others, and value the success of the team over personal glory. Through lessons on sacrifice, selflessness, and forgiveness, you will learn how to create a lasting impact both on and off the field by reflecting Christ in every interaction.

CHAPTER 10: TEAMWORK & UNITY

36

ONE TEAM, ONE MISSION

""Whatever happens, conduct yourselves in a manner worthy of the gospel of Christ. Then, whether I come and see you or only hear about you in my absence, I will know that you stand firm in the one Spirit, striving together as one for the faith of the gospel."

Philippians 1:27

BEYOND THE SCOREBOARD

Lesson: Nebraska Volleyball is one of the most decorated programs in college sports, but what makes them truly special isn't just the banners hanging in their arena—it's the unity that defines them on and off the court. Known for their culture of selflessness, discipline, and shared faith, the Huskers have built a legacy on the belief that every point, practice, and prayer matters when done together.

Instead of chasing personal stats, players are taught to prioritize "we over me." This shows up in the way they celebrate teammates' big plays just as much as their own, or how they push each other in practice to be better every single day. Their commitment goes beyond volleyball. They regularly gather in prayer circles, lifting up one another and remembering that their mission isn't only to win games but to reflect Christ in how they live and compete.

Philippians 1:27 reminds us that our lives should be worthy of the gospel and that we are called to strive together as one. This means refusing to let selfishness divide the team. Nebraska's example shows us what happens when players are united under one mission: they build trust, they play fearless, and they impact more than the scoreboard. For young female athletes, this devotion is a reminder that your mission is bigger than yourself—it's about glorifying God by playing as one team with one mission.

GAME PLAN FOR GROWTH

Reflection: *Do I look for ways to build up my teammates as much as myself? How can I show unity and humility this week in practice or competition?*

Challenge: This week, encourage a teammate with a word of affirmation or prayer. Look for one way to put the team's mission above your own goals.

FAITH HUDDLE

Prayer: Lord, thank You for the gift of teammates who make me stronger. Teach me to play with unity and to put our mission in Christ above myself. Help me bring a spirit of togetherness to every practice and game. **Amen.**

37

HEARTS HUDDLED IN CHRIST

"For where two or three gather in my name, there am I with them."

Matthew 18:20

Lesson: The University of Oklahoma softball team has become one of the most dominant dynasties in college sports. But their true strength doesn't just come from home runs or strikeouts—it comes from their unity in Christ. Before and after games, the Sooners often huddle together in prayer circles, not just to ask for wins, but to thank God for the chance to compete and to seek His presence in every inning.

Players like Jocelyn Alo and Grace Lyons have openly credited their faith as the anchor of their success. They point to the deeper mission behind the team's culture: to glorify God, play for each other, and keep God's perspective when the pressure is high. Their boldness in speaking about Jesus in press conferences has shown the world that their identity isn't built on championship wins but on their team's faith. Their coach has also emphasized that this unity isn't only about winning—it's about building a family of women who support one another through highs and lows.

Matthew 18:20 reminds us that when even two or three believers gather in His name, His presence is there. For Oklahoma softball, those huddles represent more than tradition—they're a declaration that Christ is the true center of their team. For young athletes, this is a powerful reminder: prayer doesn't have to be long or fancy. Simply gathering with teammates in God's name invites His Spirit into your game.

GAME PLAN FOR GROWTH

Reflection: *When was the last time I prayed with my teammates? How might team prayer change the way we play together?*

Challenge: Start or join a prayer circle with your team before practice or competition this week. Even if it's just a short prayer, watch how God uses unity to strengthen your hearts and transform your sport.

FAITH HUDDLE

Prayer: God, thank You for the gift of teammates and the chance to share faith together. Remind me that prayer unites hearts and draws us closer to You in everything we do. **Amen.**

38

SISTERS OVER SELF

"Be devoted to one another in love. Honor one another above yourselves."
Romans 12:10

Lesson: The **Baylor University Women's Basketball team** has built more than a powerhouse program—they've built a legacy of selfless, Christ-centered unity. During their national championship run, what stood out wasn't just their defense or rebounding—it was their relentless commitment to each other. Led by players like Chloe Jackson and Kalani Brown, the team leaned on trust, shared faith, and sacrificial play to reach the top.

Chloe Jackson, who transferred in for just one season, didn't expect to lead. But when the team needed a point guard, she humbly accepted the challenge. She stepped into an unfamiliar role, not for the spotlight, but for the good of the team. That year, she ended up hitting the game-winning shot in the national championship. Her unselfishness became the spark Baylor needed. "We all play for each other," Chloe said after the game. "It's never about me—it's about us."

Romans 12:10 calls us to honor one another above ourselves. That's what sisterhood on the court looks like: diving for each other, passing up the shot to create a better one, cheering from the bench without envy. Baylor's team culture of humility, prayer, and servant leadership reminds us that when we put Christ and teammates first, incredible things happen. True champions know that playing for the sister next to you is always greater than playing for yourself.

GAME PLAN FOR GROWTH

Reflection: *How can you serve or support a teammate this week, even if it doesn't benefit you directly? What does it mean to you to play as "sisters over self"?*

_____

_____

_____

Challenge: This week, write a short encouragement note or send a prayer to one teammate. Whether she's struggling or shining, show her what it looks like to love with Christ-like humility and put others first.

FAITH HUDDLE

Prayer: Thank You, Jesus, for giving me teammates to grow with. Help me to love them well, serve with joy, and honor others above myself on and off the court. Make me a true sister in Christ. **Amen.**

CHAPTER 11: LEADERSHIP & INFLUENCE

39

LIGHT THE WAY

"Let your light shine before others, that they may see your good deeds and glorify your Father in heaven."
Matthew 5:16

Lesson: Leadership isn't about chasing attention—it's about reflecting light. Olympic snowboarder **Kelly Clark**, a five-time U.S. Olympian and gold medalist, led not just with incredible talent but with the steady glow of her faith in Christ. Though she became one of the most accomplished snowboarders in history, what stood out even more was her humility, encouragement, and the quiet way she shaped those around her.

Her faith journey began when she overheard another rider say, *"God still loves you even if you don't win."* That simple phrase planted a seed that grew into a new perspective and a life changed by Jesus. From then on, Kelly carried herself differently by mentoring younger athletes, celebrating others' victories, and choosing peace in the middle of competition.

Matthew 5:16 reminds us that our light isn't for personal applause. It's to point people toward God's goodness. Kelly lived that out by letting her faith shine through her actions, proving that influence comes not from the medals you earn but from your character and morals.

As a young athlete, remember: your light isn't measured by stats or trophies, but by the way you treat others. When you practice humility, serve your team, and encourage others, you're leading and influencing in the most powerful way—by shining Christ's light.

GAME PLAN FOR GROWTH

Reflection: *How do my words and actions reflect Christ to others? What's one way I can shine for God in my sport this week?*

_____

_____

_____

Challenge: Lead through your light this week. Choose one intentional act of encouragement—whether cheering for a teammate, helping a struggling student, or developing a younger athlete—and let it reflect Christ, not yourself.

FAITH HUDDLE

Prayer: God, thank You for placing Your light in me. Teach me to lead through humility and kindness so others notice You, not me. Let my every action on and off the field glorify You. **Amen.**

40

ANCHOR THE TEAM

"Be shepherds of God's flock that is under your care, watching over them—not because you must, but because you are willing... not lording it over those entrusted to you, but being examples to the flock."
1 Peter 5:2–3

BEYOND THE SCOREBOARD

Lesson: True captains don't just organize plays—they inspire purpose in other. Olympic bobsledder **Elana Meyers Taylor** is one of the most decorated women in her sport with five Olympic medals. Yet her greatest legacy may not be her podium finishes, but the way she has led and anchored her team with conviction, courage, humility, and faith.

As captain of Team USA, Elana modeled what it means to serve first. She was known for pushing the sled harder, training longer, and supporting new teammates without hesitation. Beyond the ice, she used her platform to advocate for equality, inclusion, and respect in athletics, even when those choices required sacrifice. As a bold follower of Christ, Elana often said she seeks to *"honor God in everything I do,"* a statement that shaped the way she led.

1 Peter 5:2–3 reminds us that leadership isn't about power or recognition, but rather about caring for those entrusted to you. Elana lived this out daily, not leading out of duty, but out of love and responsibility before God.

For Christian athletes, anchoring the team means stepping up when it's tough, setting the tone for your team, and showing humility and heart in every moment. Leadership isn't about winning titles—it's about serving others, making sacrifices for the greater good, and pointing your teammates to Christ.

GAME PLAN FOR GROWTH

Reflection: *What example am I setting for my teammates? Do I serve others first, or do I wait to be noticed? How can I shepherd my team with humility this week?*

Challenge: Lead in a quiet but meaningful way this week. Encourage a struggling teammate, help set up equipment, or take time to pray for someone on your team. Let your actions speak louder than words.

FAITH HUDDLE

Prayer: Heavenly Father, thank You for the opportunity to lead and be an example for others. Teach me to serve with humility, guide with courage, and carry out the mission You've given me. Let my influence always point back to You. **Amen.**

41

NO ROOM FOR DRAMA

"If it is possible, as far as it depends on you, live at peace with everyone."
Romans 12:18

BEYOND THE SCOREBOARD

Lesson: On the U.S. Women's National Soccer Team, **Tobin Heath** became known not only for her creativity and composure on the field, but also for her steady presence off it. In a world where locker room drama, rivalries, jealousy, comparisons, and social media pressure can easily tear a team apart, Tobin consistently chose a different path. She openly shared that her identity rests in Christ, which allowed her to rise above petty conflicts and keep her focus on team unity and purpose.

Romans 12:18 reminds us to *"live at peace with everyone."* Female athletes, that means resisting the temptation to fuel gossip, comparison, or cliques within your team. It doesn't mean avoiding conflict at all costs, but choosing to respond in a way that reflects God's peace. Tobin modeled this by encouraging all teammates, investing in genuine friendships, and redirecting conversations away from negativity. Even when surrounded by tension, she chose to honor Christ with her positive words and selfless actions.

Tobin models Romans 12:18. She shows that leadership isn't about having the loudest voice, but about creating peace and protecting team unity. Her example offers hope to all young female athletes—you can be competitive without being combative. When you refuse to entertain drama, you make space for trust, focus, and team unity.

GAME PLAN FOR GROWTH

Reflection: *What does leading like Jesus look like in my daily actions? How can I encourage unity within my team and diffuse any team drama or negativity? Who in my life might God be calling me to mentor or influence for Him?*

Challenge: This week, practice servant leadership. Look for one opportunity to put someone else's needs above your own by quietly serving behind the scenes. Lead through example, not attention.

FAITH HUDDLE

Prayer: God, thank You for placing me on a team where I can grow both in my sport and in my faith. Help me lead with peace, resist drama, and reflect Your love in every word and action. **Amen.**

42

LEAD LIKE JESUS

"Follow my example, as I follow the example of Christ."
1 Corinthians 11:1

Lesson: Natasha Watley is one of the most decorated softball players in America—an Olympic gold and silver medalist, a trailblazer for women in her sport, and a role model for countless young female athletes. But what sets Natasha apart isn't only her skill on the diamond, it's the way she chose to lead with service, humility, and Christ-centered influence.

After her playing career, Natasha founded the Natasha Watley Foundation, where she mentors young girls by teaching them softball skills, confidence, and values rooted in faith. For Natasha, leadership has never been about standing above others. It's about walking alongside them and lifting them up. Her vision reflects the heart of 1 Corinthians 11:1, which calls us to follow Christ's example and lead others by pointing them toward Him.

Natasha's story shows that true leadership is not about power, recognition, or the number of medals you have, but about modeling Jesus' servant heart. She didn't keep her success to herself. She used it to impact the next generation, showing them that their worth and purpose come from God. For young female athletes, this is encouragement to see leadership not as a title, but as an opportunity to influence teammates, classmates, and friends for Christ. Leading like Jesus means serving first, mentoring with humility, and letting your example shine brighter than your words.

GAME PLAN FOR GROWTH

Reflection: *How can I lead like Jesus in my daily actions? How can I encourage or serve a teammate this week?*

Challenge: Practice servant leadership this week. Look for one opportunity to put a teammate's needs above your own or quietly serving behind the scenes. Lead through example, not attention.

FAITH HUDDLE

Prayer: God, thank You for giving me leaders who point me toward Christ. Teach me to lead with humility, serve with joy, and influence others by following the example of Jesus. May my leadership always reflect You. **Amen.**

CHAPTER 12: SACRIFICE & SELFLESSNESS

43

GREATER THAN ME

"For to me, to live is Christ and to die is gain."
Philippians 1:21

BEYOND THE SCOREBOARD

Lesson: When most athletes chase numbers and recognition, **Kenzie Koerber** pursued something higher—God's calling. She was already a standout in college volleyball, earning All-American honors and Pac-12 Player of the Year. Yet her boldest move wasn't about staying in the spotlight. After a decorated career at Utah, she transferred to BYU—not for more exposure, but to deepen her faith and surround herself with teammates who shared her mission. Kenzie willingly stepped away from her comfort zone because she knew following Christ was greater than chasing applause.

Philippians 1:21 captures that heart: to live is to follow Christ in everything. Kenzie didn't just wear that verse on a wristband—she lived it. At BYU, she became a mentor to younger players and an encourager in the locker room. Her identity wasn't defined by kills, digs, or stats, but by her faith in Jesus. Whether celebrating a win or supporting a teammate in struggle, she pointed others back to Him.

This is what living *greater than me* looks like. It's not about shrinking your ambition, but reshaping it—using every practice, every huddle, every moment to reflect Christ. For female athletes, Kenzie's story shows that influence goes far beyond trophies. True greatness comes when you choose God's mission over your own spotlight.

GAME PLAN FOR GROWTH

Reflection: *Where have I made my sport about me instead of God? How can I use my role to serve a greater purpose? What would "greater than me" look like in my season right now?*

Challenge: This week, take one step that lifts up a teammate instead of yourself—help someone improve their skills, celebrate their success, or encourage them after a tough moment. Let your actions declare: "I'm here for more than me."

FAITH HUDDLE

Prayer: Heavenly Father, thank You for calling me to something greater than myself. Help me put You first, serve my teammates with humility, and use my sport as a way to glorify You. **Amen.**

44

SURRENDER THE SPOTLIGHT

"Do nothing out of selfish ambition or vain conceit. Rather, in humility value others above yourselves."
Philippians 2:3

BEYOND THE SCOREBOARD

Lesson: In the high-pressure world of Olympic volleyball, **Courtney Thompson** became known not for chasing the spotlight but for how she gave it away. As a two-time Olympian and key member of Team USA, Courtney's leadership was rarely about being the star. She embraced the role of setter—a position built on creating opportunities for others to shine. Every perfect set she delivered was an act of selflessness, proving that greatness can be found in lifting teammates higher.

Philippians 2:3 challenges us to resist the pull of selfish ambition and instead choose humility. Courtney lived this out on and off the court. She consistently credited her teammates, praised their effort, and carried an attitude of joy even when she wasn't the one finishing the play. In interviews, she often reminded others that volleyball is a team game, and her mission was to make those around her better.

Her story reminds us that surrendering the spotlight doesn't mean shrinking back. It means knowing your role and embracing it with humility. This is a call to value others above yourself, whether you're scoring points or cheering from the sidelines. True influence isn't about who gets the attention but about who helps others reach their best.

GAME PLAN FOR GROWTH

Reflection: *When have I wanted the spotlight instead of sharing it? How can I encourage my teammates to shine this week? Do I see my role as valuable, even if it isn't noticed?*

Challenge: At your next practice or game, choose one way to give a teammate the spotlight—set them up for success, cheer their name, or celebrate their win as if it were your own.

FAITH HUDDLE

Prayer: My Lord, thank You for teaching me that selflessness is strength. Help me surrender the spotlight, lift others higher, and find joy in serving my team with a selfless heart. **Amen.**

45

SACRIFICE TO LIFT OTHERS

"Greater love has no one than this: to lay down one's life for one's friends."
John 15:13

Lesson: Few athletes have lived out the power of sacrifice like **Allyson Felix**. Known as the most decorated American track and field sprinter, her legacy goes far beyond medals. In 2018, when Allyson became a mother, she confronted a painful truth: many elite female athletes were financially penalized or even dropped from contracts when starting families. Instead of staying silent to protect her own career, she risked everything to challenge Nike's policies, sacrificing endorsements and security to fight for women's rights in sports.

John 15:13 calls us to the highest form of love—laying something down for others. Sacrifice isn't always about giving your life; sometimes it's about giving up comfort, status, or opportunity so someone else can thrive. Allyson's stand cost her millions in sponsorships, but her courage brought change for countless future female athletes. Later, she partnered with

Athleta and launched her own brand of shoes, proving that God can use sacrifice to build something greater than we could imagine.

Allyson's story is a reminder that being a champion isn't just about podiums. It's about how you use your influence for others. Sacrifice might look like cheering for the teammate who gets more playing time, helping someone else improve, or speaking truth when it's unpopular. True greatness is found in giving, not just winning.

GAME PLAN FOR GROWTH

Reflection: *Am I willing to give something up to help someone else? In what ways can I sacrifice for my teammates this week? Do I play more for myself, or for the greater good of my team?*

Challenge: Find one chance this week to serve someone else at your own expense—encourage a struggling teammate, give up your time to help them train, or celebrate their win as if it were your own.

FAITH HUDDLE

Prayer: Lord, thank You for showing us perfect love through Jesus' sacrifice. Help me to live with that same selfless spirit, to put others before myself, and to use my influence for good. Teach me to lift others higher. **Amen.**

SECTION IV: LIVING LIKE CHRIST

(WEEKS 46 - 52)

Your legacy as a female athlete isn't just about stats alone. It's about how you reflect Christ in everything you do. This set of devotions challenges all female athletes to live boldly, forgive quickly, and lead with humility, even when no one is watching. You will discover, through powerful examples of grace, forgiveness, sacrifice, and unshakable faith, how to be a light for Christ in your sport—becoming a faithful witness through the way you speak, act, and carry yourself far beyond your sport.

CHAPTER 13: GRACE & FORGIVENESS

46

GRACE IN DEFEAT

"I can do all this through him who gives me strength."
Philippians 4:13

BEYOND THE SCOREBOARD

Lesson: Even the greatest athletes face defeats, and how they respond reveals their true character. **Serena Williams**, one of the most dominant tennis players in the world, has experienced both incredible triumphs and painful losses on the world stage. After her shocking defeat in the 2018 U.S. Open final, instead of focusing on disappointment, Serena showed grace by congratulating her opponent, Naomi Osaka. She also encouraged the crowd to celebrate Naomi's victory in her own defeat. In interviews after other tough matches, Serena has often pointed to her faith, saying: *"I am not the one who has been given this amazing ability. God has chosen me, and I am just blessed to be able to do what I do."*

Philippians 4:13 reminds us that strength isn't just for winning—it's for staying grounded when we fall short. To live out this verse means relying on God for composure in the hardest moments, not just confidence in victory. Serena demonstrates that kind of strength. She doesn't crumble when defeated; instead, she leans on God and her faith and displays humility and grace.

This is a powerful lesson for young female athletes: your legacy isn't just about the trophies you accumulate but more importantly about your heart when things don't go your way. Wins may build your reputation, but grace in defeat builds your character. When you respond with humility, gratitude, and respect, you shine even brighter for Christ.

GAME PLAN FOR GROWTH

Reflection: *When I lose or fail, do I respond with humility or frustration? How can I rely on God's strength to show grace in defeat?*

Challenge: This week, after a loss or big mistake, choose one positive action: thank a coach, congratulate a teammate, or pray for your opponent. Let your response reflect your strength in Christ, not frustration.

FAITH HUDDLE

Prayer: Father, thank You for giving me strength in every circumstance. Teach me to show humility when I fall short and to respond with grace and gratitude. Help me trust Your plan for me in both victory and defeat. **Amen.**

47

STRONGER THAN THE STUMBLE

"For though the righteous fall seven times, they rise again."
Proverbs 24:16

Lesson: Falling short is one of the hardest moments for any athlete. **Erin Jackson**, one of the world's fastest speedskaters, experienced this on the biggest stage. At the 2022 U.S. Olympic trials, she stumbled during her race and lost her spot on the team. For a moment, everything she had trained for seemed gone. But God had a bigger plan for her. In one of the greatest acts of selflessness, Jackson's teammate Brittany Bowe gave up her own spot so Erin could compete. Erin didn't let the previous stumble define her—she rose to the occasion. Weeks later, she made history as the first Black woman to win an Olympic gold medal in speedskating.

Proverbs 24:16 tells us, *"For though the righteous fall seven times, they rise again."* This verse isn't about avoiding mistakes—it's about how you respond to your mistakes and setbacks. With God's strength, we can rise, recover, and keep moving forward. Erin's stumble didn't end her journey; it became the setup for a greater victory.

For female athletes, it's important to understand that stumbles will happen. There will be times when you'll miss shots, lose races, or fall short of expectations. But failure doesn't define who you are—your response does. Rising above the mistakes with faith, humility, and resilience shows true strength. Like Erin, you can trust God's plan, keep your eyes forward, and let Him turn setbacks into powerful comebacks.

GAME PLAN FOR GROWTH

Reflection: *When I make mistakes in my sport, do I focus on the failure or the comeback? How can I remind myself that God defines my worth, not my stumbles? What's one way I can "rise again" this week after a setback?*

Challenge: When you stumble—whether in practice, competition, or daily life—pause, take a deep breath, and remind yourself of Proverbs 24:16. Write down one positive step you'll take to rise again stronger than before.

FAITH HUDDLE

Prayer: Father, thank You for giving me the courage to rise again. Help me see every stumble as a chance to grow stronger and trust You more. Keep my heart steady and my eyes fixed on You, not the stumbles. **Amen.**

48

FEARLESS TO FORGIVE

"Bear with each other and forgive one another if any of you has a grievance against someone. Forgive as the Lord forgave you."
Colossians 3:13

BEYOND THE SCOREBOARD

Lesson: In her rookie WNBA season, **Caitlin Clark** faced pressure few young athletes could imagine. Every game brought massive attention, sold-out arenas, and defenders eager to test her toughness—mentally and physically. At times, the physical play crossed the line—hard fouls, cold shoulders, and critics waiting for her to crack. Instead of responding with anger or resentment, Caitlin chose to stay composed. *"I'm focused on learning, staying composed, and letting my game speak,"* she explained in an interview. Her poise became just as powerful as her three-point shot.

Colossians 3:13 reminds us that forgiveness is not optional—it's the call of every Christian believer. To *"forgive as the Lord forgave you"* means extending patience and grace even when it feels undeserved. For Caitlin, that has meant not retaliating when provoked and refusing to be defined by bitterness. Forgiveness isn't weakness—it's strength under control.

Caitlin's example shows young female athletes that forgiveness often plays out in the heat of the moment: when a foul feels unfair, when words sting, or when pressure builds. Forgiveness frees you to focus on your purpose instead of being trapped by anger.

Like Caitlin, you don't have to be fearless in talent alone. You can be fearless in forgiving. When you release grudges, you rise above drama and show the power of Christ at work in your heart.

GAME PLAN FOR GROWTH

Reflection: *How do I respond when I feel disrespected in my sport? What does it look like to forgive in the moment, not just later? Who is one person I need to release bitterness toward this week?*

Challenge: When someone frustrates you—on or off the court—pause before reacting. Whisper Colossians 3:13 to yourself, and choose the higher ground of forgiveness. Respond with composure that points others to Christ instead of adding fuel to the conflict.

FAITH HUDDLE

Prayer: Lord, thank You for forgiving me completely through Jesus. Teach me to show that same fearless forgiveness to others, even when it's hard. Help me respond with grace that shines Your love in every game and moment. **Amen.**

CHAPTER 14: WITNESS & CHRIST-LIKE CHARACTER

49

DIFFERENT BY DESIGN

"Do not conform to the pattern of this world, but be transformed by the renewing of your mind."
Romans 12:2

Lesson: Jennie Finch, Olympic gold medalist and one of the most famous softball players in the world, built her career not just on strikeouts, but on standing out for Christ. While many athletes chase popularity, endorsements, and the spotlight, Jennie boldly chose to live differently. She wore her faith openly, pointing to Jesus in interviews, signing autographs with Bible verses, and mentoring younger athletes to play with eternal purpose. Her impact didn't stop at the medals—she became a role model who showed girls that you can compete fiercely and still honor God with humility.

Romans 12:2 calls us not to conform to the world's standards, but to be transformed by Christ. For Jennie, this meant saying no to the pressure to fit in with cultural norms, and yes to reflecting God's character on and off the field. She showed that true greatness isn't just about stats, but more about living out her faith differently than the norm.

Jennie's influence continues today as she speaks at faith events, coaches young athletes, and encourages girls to find their worth in Christ instead of comparison. Her life reminds us that you don't need to follow the world's pattern to make an impact—you just need to follow Christ. When you live differently by design, you shine in ways that change teammates, teams, and generations.

GAME PLAN FOR GROWTH

Reflection: *Where do I feel pressure to "fit in" with the world's pattern in sports or school? What would it look like to live differently for Christ instead? How can I use my platform to point others to Him?*

Challenge: This week, choose one way to live "different by design." It could be praying before practice, sharing encouragement with a teammate, or responding with kindness when others wouldn't. Let your actions reflect Christ's transformation in you.

FAITH HUDDLE

Prayer: God, thank You for designing me to live differently by design. Help me resist the pressure to conform and instead reflect You in my words, actions, and attitude. May my life point others to You in every game and moment. **Amen.**

50

SHINE UNASHAMED

"For I am not ashamed of the gospel, because it is the power of God that brings salvation to everyone who believes."
Romans 1:16

BEYOND THE SCOREBOARD

Lesson: Gabby Douglas made history as the first African American gymnast to win the Olympic all-around gold medal, but her impact reaches far beyond medals. In the bright lights of the London and Rio Olympics, Gabby never hid her faith. She openly spoke about reading her Bible daily, praying before competitions, and giving all glory to God after routines. Even when she faced harsh criticism from media and fans—comments about her hair, her smile, and her performance—Gabby stood firm. She refused to let negativity dim her light or make her shrink back from sharing her faith.

Romans 1:16 reminds us that we are called to be unashamed of the gospel. For Gabby, this meant giving credit to God in the middle of the world's biggest stage, even when the media questioned or mocked her. She showed that courage isn't just about sticking a perfect landing—it's more about standing boldly for Christ when it's unpopular.

Young athletes can take heart from Gabby's example. You don't have to hide your faith to fit in. When you stand firm in Christ, your confidence shines brighter than criticism. Gabby proves that real victory isn't just winning medals. It's representing Jesus with courage, confidence, and boldness. That's the kind of shine the world can't ignore.

GAME PLAN FOR GROWTH

Reflection: *When have I felt pressure to hide my faith around teammates or friends? What would it look like for me to live unashamed of Jesus this week? How can I give God the glory in my sport?*

Challenge: Find one opportunity this week to boldly live out your faith—pray before a game, share a Bible verse with a teammate, or simply thank God out loud for a win or a loss. Let others see who fuels your light.

FAITH HUDDLE

Prayer: Dear God, thank You for the example of Gabby Douglas and her courage to shine unashamed. Please give me the same boldness to live out my faith in every arena of life. May my confidence point others to You. **Amen.**

51

WITNESS ON THE FIELD

"But you will receive power when the Holy Spirit comes on you; and you will be my witnesses in Jerusalem, and in all Judea and Samaria, and to the ends of the earth."
Acts 1:8

BEYOND THE SCOREBOARD

Lesson: When the world is watching, **Alyssa Naeher** doesn't just play—she witnesses for God. As goalkeeper for the U.S. Women's National Soccer Team, she has faced some of the most intense moments in sports history. From penalty shootouts in World Cups to Olympic matches, Alyssa's calm presence has anchored her team. Yet what truly sets her apart is her quiet faith. After clutch performances, she often points upward, giving the glory to God before she celebrates with teammates.

Acts 1:8 reminds us that every believer is called to be a witness, wherever God places them. For Alyssa, the soccer field becomes her mission field. She doesn't need a microphone to testify; her composure, humility, and faith-filled actions speak louder than words. She shows female athletes that being a witness isn't just preaching the Gospel—it's living boldly and differently so others see Christ through you.

Alyssa's example encourages female athletes to remember that your sport isn't separate from your faith. Whether in practice or under stadium lights, you have opportunities to reflect Christ by how you treat teammates, handle pressure, and give glory where it's due. Alyssa proves that being a witness for Christ isn't about being perfect. No one is perfect. It's about being consistent in reflecting Christ in everything you do.

GAME PLAN FOR GROWTH

Reflection: *How can I treat my practices and games as opportunities to be a witness for Christ? What qualities of a true witness—humility, gratitude, love—do I want to show this week?*

_____

_____

_____

Challenge: As you go about your week, look for one opportunity to reflect Christ through your actions on the field, whether it's encouraging a discouraged teammate, handling a mistake with grace, or publicly giving God the glory.

FAITH HUDDLE

Prayer: Lord, thank You for placing me in my sport where I can be a witness for You. Help me live and compete with humility, courage, and faith so others can see Jesus through me. **Amen.**

52

HUMBLE IN GREATNESS

"Humble yourselves before the Lord, and he will lift you up."
James 4:10

BEYOND THE SCOREBOARD

Lesson: Katie Ledecky is one of the most decorated swimmers in history of the sport, with multiple Olympic gold medals and world records that may never be broken. But what makes Katie's story so remarkable isn't just the records—it's how she carries herself. Despite being called the greatest female swimmer of all time, Katie constantly points away from herself and toward God, with gratitude and humility. After races, she's quick to thank God, her coaches, and her teammates before she ever mentions her own accomplishments.

James 4:10 reminds us that true greatness isn't about standing the tallest—it's about bowing the lowest before God. Katie's humility is evidence of this truth. She has said, *"All I can do is my best, and let God handle the rest,"* reflecting her unwavering trust that her identity isn't in medals, but in Christ. Even in dominating victories, she demonstrates grace and composure, reminding the world that greatness is about reflecting Christ-like character, not just achievement.

For young athletes, Katie's example proves that being the best doesn't mean boasting or bragging the loudest. It means recognizing that every gift, every win, and every opportunity to succeed comes from God. Her legacy isn't only her records—it's her Christlike character. Humility in greatness is powerful, because it shows that success is safest in the hands of those who know Who gave it.

GAME PLAN FOR GROWTH

Reflection: *How can I stay humble even when I succeed? What's one way I can give God glory instead of taking it for myself?*

_____

_____

_____

Challenge: The next time you succeed—whether in practice, school, or competition—redirect the spotlight. Thank a coach, a teammate, or God first. Choose humility over hype.

FAITH HUDDLE

Prayer: Father, thank You for the example of Katie Ledecky. Teach me that true greatness comes through humility, grace, and gratitude. Teach me to give You glory in every success and stay grounded in Christ above all else. **Amen.**

YOUR LEGACY STARTS HERE

You've reached the last devotion, but this is far from the final whistle. Week by week, you trained your heart, strengthened your faith, and discovered what it means to compete with a higher purpose. This devotional wasn't about earning a medal or checking a box—it was about becoming the kind of athlete who shines for Christ on and off the field. True greatness isn't measured only by wins or stats. It's measured in the way you lead, encourage, serve, forgive, persevere, and worship through your sport. That's what makes you stand out as a female athlete amongst your peers.

You've read stories of women who pushed through pressure, bounced back from setbacks, overcame self-confidence issues, and boldly gave God the glory in both victory and defeat. They weren't superstars overnight. What carried them higher wasn't just their talent, it was their unshakable faith.

As in sports, one season ends so another can begin. Let this be a reminder that your faith is your greatest advantage. Keep chasing the athlete God designed you to be. Open your Bible before you lace up. Pray before each game. Encourage the teammate who's struggling and compete with integrity, even when nobody's watching.

Let this devotional be the start of your legacy—not your finish.

SCRIPTURE SOURCES

Throughout this devotional, Scripture verses have been drawn from multiple Bible translations to bring clarity and impact to each lesson. The following translations were used: New International Version (NIV), English Standard Version (ESV), and New Living Translation (NLT). Each verse has been carefully chosen to communicate biblical truth in a way that resonates with today's female athletes. Used by permission. All rights reserved.

Biblica, Inc. (2011). *The Holy Bible: New International Version*. (Original work published 1973). Biblica, Inc.

Crossway. (2001). *The Holy Bible: English Standard Version*. Crossway Bibles.

Tyndale House Foundation. (2015). *The Holy Bible: New Living Translation*. (Original work published 1996). Tyndale House Publishers, Inc.

www.ingramcontent.com/pod-product-compliance
Lightning Source LLC
Chambersburg PA
CBHW061649120626
46550CB00003B/883